# A Healing Homiletic

## Preaching and Disability

### KATHY BLACK

ABINGDON PRESS
Nashville

A HEALING HOMILETIC
PREACHING AND DISABILITY

Copyright © 1996 by Abingdon Press

*This book is printed on acid-free, elemental chlorine-free, recycled paper.*

**Library of Congress Cataloging-in-Publication Data**

Black, Kathy.
    A healing homiletic : preaching and disability / by Kathy Black.
        p.   cm.
    Includes bibliographical references and index.
    ISBN 0-687-00291-5 (pbk. : alk. paper)
    1. Jesus Christ—Miracles.  2. Spiritual healing.  3. Preaching.
    4. Handicapped—Religious aspects—Christianity.  I. Title.
BT366.B58  1996
261.8'324—dc20                                                    96-30770
                                                                       CIP

96 97 98 99 00 01 02 03 04 05—-10 9 8 7 6 5 4 3 2 1

MANUFACTURED IN THE UNITED STATES OF AMERICA

*In loving honor of my parents,*

Gwyneth and George Black

# Contents

Preface. . . . . . . . . . . . . . . . . . . . . . . . . . . . . . . . . . . . . . . . . . . . . . . 7

Acknowledgments. . . . . . . . . . . . . . . . . . . . . . . . . . . . . . . . . . . . 10

Introduction . . . . . . . . . . . . . . . . . . . . . . . . . . . . . . . . . . . . . . . . 11

**Part I**

*Chapter One:* Healing and Theodicy . . . . . . . . . . . . . . . . . . . . . 19
    Angel or Devil, Blessed or Cursed. . . . . . . . . . . . . . . . . . . 20
    God's Will . . . . . . . . . . . . . . . . . . . . . . . . . . . . . . . . . . . . . . 23
        Punishment for Sin. . . . . . . . . . . . . . . . . . . . . . . . . . 23
        A Test of Faith . . . . . . . . . . . . . . . . . . . . . . . . . . . . . 25
        Opportunity for Character Development. . . . . . . . . 27
        Manifestation of the Power of God . . . . . . . . . . . . 29
        Redemptive Suffering. . . . . . . . . . . . . . . . . . . . . . . . 30
        God's Mysterious Omnipotence . . . . . . . . . . . . . . . 32
    A Theology of Interdependence . . . . . . . . . . . . . . . . . . . . 34

*Chapter Two:* Hermeneutical Hazards. . . . . . . . . . . . . . . . . . . 43
    Bridging the Gap . . . . . . . . . . . . . . . . . . . . . . . . . . . . . . . 44
        Medical Values: Now and Then . . . . . . . . . . . . . . . 45
        Sickness, Disease, and Illness. . . . . . . . . . . . . . . . . 47
        Cure and Healing . . . . . . . . . . . . . . . . . . . . . . . . . . 50
    Metaphorical Interpretations . . . . . . . . . . . . . . . . . . . . . 54

**Part II**

*Chapter Three:* Blindness . . . . . . . . . . . . . . . . . . . . . . . . . . . . . 57
    Blindness . . . . . . . . . . . . . . . . . . . . . . . . . . . . . . . . . . . . . 58
        The Text: John 9:1-41 . . . . . . . . . . . . . . . . . . . . . . . 60
        Hermeneutics . . . . . . . . . . . . . . . . . . . . . . . . . . . . . 64
        Traditional Homiletic . . . . . . . . . . . . . . . . . . . . . . . 75
        A Healing Homiletic . . . . . . . . . . . . . . . . . . . . . . . . 77
        The Text: Mark 10:46-52 . . . . . . . . . . . . . . . . . . . . 78
        Hermeneutics . . . . . . . . . . . . . . . . . . . . . . . . . . . . . 78
        Traditional Homiletic . . . . . . . . . . . . . . . . . . . . . . . 85
        A Healing Homiletic . . . . . . . . . . . . . . . . . . . . . . . . 86

*Chapter Four:* Deafness and Hearing Loss . . . . . . . . . . . . . . . 88
    Deafness and Hearing Loss. . . . . . . . . . . . . . . . . . . . . . . 88

# CONTENTS

The Text: Mark 7:31-37 .......................... 92
   Hermeneutics ............................... 93
   Traditional Homiletic ......................... 99
   A Healing Homiletic ......................... 102

*Chapter Five:* Paralysis ............................. 104
   Paralysis ......................................... 104
   The Text: Mark 2:1-12 ....................... 109
   Hermeneutics ............................. 110
   Traditional Homiletic ........................ 118
   A Healing Homiletic ......................... 120

*Chapter Six:* Leprosy and Chronic Illness ................. 124
   Ritual Purity Laws ............................. 125
   Leprosy in Biblical Times ....................... 129
   The Text: Mark 1:40-45 ....................... 131
   Hermeneutics ............................. 132
   Traditional Homiletic ........................ 137
   A Healing Homiletic ......................... 139
   The Text: Luke 17:11-19 ...................... 141
   Hermeneutics ............................. 141
   Traditional Homiletic ........................ 145
   A Healing Homiletic ......................... 147
   Chronic Illness ............................... 148
   The Text: Mark 5:25-34 ....................... 151
   Hermeneutics ............................. 152
   Traditional Homiletic ........................ 156
   A Healing Homiletic ......................... 157

*Chapter Seven:* Mental Illness ......................... 159
   Demon Possession in Biblical Times .............. 160
   Mental Illness ................................ 162
   The Text: Luke 8:26-39 ....................... 165
   Hermeneutics ............................. 167
   Traditional Homiletic ........................ 175
   A Healing Homiletic ......................... 177

*Chapter Eight:* A Healing Homilectic .................... 180

Notes ............................................. 187

Scripture Index .................................... 198

# Preface

I have been ruminating over the contents of this book for many years. As a weekly churchgoer from infancy on and now as a homiletics professor, I have heard a lot of sermons in my time. And each time I hear a sermon on one of the Bible's many healing narratives, there is something inside of me that is greatly discomforted. It is this sense of discomfort and its origins that I have tried to articulate in this book.

As I have worked with persons with various disabilities over the years, I have wondered how they react to what is preached about biblical characters with similar disabilities. In my early college years I worked with our local United Methodist Women's group to teach independent living skills to one of our youth group members who was blind. In my later college years I did recreational therapy at a Cerebral Palsy Center and then worked for the Commission on the Blind of New Jersey at a preschool for children who were both deaf and blind. The deafness and blindness of most of the children at the school was the result of one of the rubella epidemics. I had had a sister who had died in infancy, and at that time we believed her death was a result of severe disabilities caused by my mother's exposure to the rubella virus while she was pregnant. I had always wondered what our lives would have been like if she had lived, and this was part of what drew me to this particular school.

During my first weeks on the job, I took a basic sign language class so that I could communicate the basics with the children: eat, bathroom, and home. I had the privilege of working with a boy there named Robbie. He was an adrenoleukodystrophy (ALD) child. The movie *Lorenzo's Oil*, based on the true story of the discovery of an effective treatment for ALD, spurred popular interest in this disease. Unfortunately, Robbie died before the oil that Lorenzo's parents isolated as a means to halt the disease was discovered. After college I went on to seminary. The day I was to be approved by my denomination for deacon's ordination was the same day I presided at my first funeral. It was for Robbie, who died at the age of eight. He had a major effect on my life and ministry.

All the families of the children at the preschool needed the comfort and support of their various faith communities. But the reality was that most often the church and its representative clergy did not know what to say or what to do. The Sunday school and nursery programs were not equipped to handle a child with a disability. The result was that the family would split up on Sunday morning. One parent would take the other children to church and Sunday school while the other would stay home with the child with the disability. When they were questioning God and their faith, when they needed the church the most, the church was not fully present for them.

During seminary I took more sign language classes at Gallaudet University, a liberal arts college for deaf students in Washington, D.C. I knew that as a pastor I could include most persons with disabilities in the life of the church, but unless I knew sign language, there would always be a barrier between me and deaf people.

After seminary, I became a chaplain at Gallaudet and the associate pastor of the Washington United Methodist Church of the Deaf. A few years later I was appointed as the founding pastor of the Magothy United Methodist Church of the Deaf in Pasadena, Maryland, and subsequently a lecturer in deaf ministry at Wesley Theological Seminary in Washington.

Clearly, all of these experiences have influenced the contents of this book. However, it has been my own personal disability that has called me to complete this task. Since the age of seven I have experienced what I thought were blackouts, fainting spells. These episodes have been more frequent and have lasted longer during some periods of my life than during others, but they have been a consistent part of my reality on at least a week-to-week basis. From the time I began the research on this book to the time of the book's completion, these episodes have become much more frequent and last for hours instead of minutes. I have also come to learn that they are not fainting spells but episodes of temporary flaccid paralysis. I cannot speak, open my eyes, or move any of my muscles, but I am fully conscious. I hear and feel.

My own experience has made me reflect all the more on issues of social stigma, people's reaction to a different mode of existence, accessibility, dependence and independence and interdependence. I've learned how frustrating planning one's schedule for the next day, let alone the next month, can be when daily existence is so very inconsistent. Most important, I've thought about all the comments people have made to me over the years trying to bring some meaning to my disability: "God must be trying to teach you something"; "I'm taking you to the faith healer in Baltimore next week"; "Your condition is so rare, medical science must be learning lots from you"; "I'm sure you'll get well soon."

I have come to realize that most of the comments that are so discomforting to me are theologically based. And much of that theology has been internalized by our contemporary society because of the way the biblical healing narratives have been preached over the centuries. This book is an attempt to look afresh at these texts from the perspective of those in the narrative who have disabilities—the people whom Jesus cures—and to ask questions about the meaning of healing in the lives of persons with disabilities today.

# Acknowledgments

Deepest thanks to Robbie Backenson and the other children at the deaf-blind preschool; the deaf students at Gallaudet University; and the members of Washington United Methodist Church of the Deaf and Magothy United Methodist Church of the Deaf. My association with them has drastically changed the direction of my life. I owe a debt of gratitude for all they have taught me.

Thanks also to those who read portions of the manuscript and offered their insight: Helen Betenbaugh, Bill Clements, Jack Coogan, Kathleen Greider, Marjorie Suchocki, and Joseph Webb. I am grateful to Julie Rees for providing hospitality in Australia, and to the Rev. Meredyth Bellows who shared her son's journey with me and allowed me to include personal narratives in the book.

I appreciate the honest struggles the students at the School of Theology at Claremont had as I tested out the material of this book in class. Some students came from communities and cultures in which disability is associated with shame or in which faith healing is the only health care available or affordable. I am grateful for their openness to new theological perspectives and homiletical approaches to the Gospel healing narratives.

As a person living with a disability, I have learned how healing an interdependent community can be from Marjorie Suchocki, Kathleen Greider, Jane Heckles, and Joan and Jim Swenson. I have experienced healing from a distance from Ida Thornton, Mary Kraus, Susan Morrison, Sandra Hale, Janie Spahr, and Edwina Hunter. The touch of my great physician Dr. Judith Moore breaks down barriers of isolation, helps me live to my fullest capacity, and brings continual healing when cure is highly improbable.

# Introduction

Last spring, a young man named Sig died. He was the twenty-four-year-old son of a United Methodist minister. Sig was born with a form of epilepsy that was never totally controlled but was being managed by medication. He became involved in a church (not United Methodist) that welcomed him warmly and included him in their fellowship. But this church preached that if he just had enough faith, he would be *healed* of his epilepsy. Encouraged to prove just how much faith he had, Sig stopped taking his medication. Soon afterward, he suffered a severe seizure and died. As his mother says, he overdosed on religion.

For the past several years, I have been struggling with the effect preaching the Gospel healing miracle stories has on persons such as Sig—persons with various disabilities. The message he heard was certainly not *healing* for him.

"Healing" is a complex term that has taken on varied meanings in religious communities over the centuries. From the biblical times until the present, healings (meaning cures) have been cited as proof of miracles. New Testament audiences saw these healing miracles of cure as sure and certain evidence that Jesus' power came from God.

Today we often have mixed feelings about "healing." We want to affirm God's ability to bring healing to the lives of those who suffer, but we also want to avoid any association with faith healers who focus solely on cure and use the suffering of others for their own power and financial gain. And yet healing ministries have been a part of the church since its beginnings. Wherever there are human beings, there

11

is suffering at various levels, and where there is suffering, we experience the need for healing. But what constitutes "healing"? What is the difference between healing and cure? What did healing mean in the context of first-century Jewish Palestine? What did healing mean within the Hellenistic cultures that nurtured early Christianity? What was the effect of Jesus' actions on the multitude of individuals with various disabilities?

Equally important are the connections we make between the biblical healing texts and our contemporary situation. What does healing mean for us today? What theologies undergird our preaching of the healing texts found in the Gospel narratives? What effect does our preaching have on those persons who live with disabilities today?

These are some of the questions this book intends to address. How we preach the healing texts contributes greatly to the theology and general attitude that laypeople have towards persons with disabilities in general. Our interpretation of these texts also contributes to the exclusion of persons with disabilities from most of our churches today.

The biblical healing texts were intended to be liberating events for those whom Jesus healed. Though they had been excluded from the worshiping community and from society at large because of their disability, Jesus' acts allowed them to be full participants in their religious, secular, and domestic spheres. The healing was liberating because it meant incorporation back into these communities.

Since that time, however, the manner in which homileticians have preached these texts is often oppressive to persons with disabilities. Intentional or not, the end result is exclusion and alienation. The liberating effects of Jesus' ministry have somehow become lost in the numerous interpretations of these texts over the centuries. The theologies and language used in our sermons often affects the disability community in a way that is the reverse of what is intended.

Both the conservative and liberal ends of the theological spectrum have contributed to the alienation and oppression of persons with disabilities. The conservative perspective tends to look at healing in terms of "cure." The healing texts are taken literally, and accordingly, persons with disabilities today need to be "cured" to be returned to "wholeness"—to be in a right relationship with God. The homiletical emphasis is on elevating Jesus and pointing out the lowly status of the person being healed. The implication is that if a person is blind, or deaf, or paralyzed, or "demon possessed," there is something wrong with the person that needs fixing: the person is in sin and requires salvation, or the person's faith is not strong enough and repentance is required.

The liberals take a more psychological approach to healing or avoid the concept of a healing ministry altogether. The healing texts in the Gospels are used metaphorically, or the healing itself is put aside so that more important issues in the text can be dealt with: the author's intent on using the story in the first place, why it was included at that particular place in the Gospel, or what the story contributed to the author's overall goal in writing the Gospel.[1]

In neither case is the person being healed in the biblical texts dealt with as a subject or agent of his or her own history. We tend to use them as objects to make some other point. The problem with this is that persons with disabilities today likewise find themselves treated as objects. Health care, education, employment, social services—all the basic institutions of our society often view persons with disabilities as objects to be dealt with, rather than as subjects that have something to contribute.

Religious institutions are no exception. Persons with disabilities often find themselves judged or excluded from contemporary faith communities. For some people, persons with disabilities represent sin and lack of faith: people who are "not whole" and therefore not "holy" enough to be present in worship. For others "they" simply do not exist. Persons with disabilities are ignored, dismissed as nonentities, and little thought is given as to why their presence is lacking within the church.

While physical barriers such as stairs and the absence of sign language interpreters also clearly exclude persons with disabilities from churches, there are other books that identify the problem and present possible solutions to this particular issue. This book, however, deals with the theological and attitudinal barriers enforced through the interpretation of healing texts in the preaching event. The purpose of this book is to analyze the healing narratives from the perspective of persons with disabilities. The individuals with disabilities from the biblical texts as well as persons with those disabilities today are treated as subjects—agents in their own right.

Part I contains two chapters that provide background material for part II. Chapter 1 deals with the various theological perspectives concerning God's relationship with persons with disabilities. Here I challenge the belief that disability is the will of God and propose a theology of interdependence. Chapter 2 discusses the two common approaches to the healing narratives: literal interpretation and metaphorical interpretation of the texts. Understanding first-century medical worldviews, concepts of sickness, illness and disease, and the difference between cure and healing will provide insights on how preachers can bridge the gap between now and then.

Part II deals with specific healing texts. While healing texts can be found in the Hebrew Bible as well as in the Acts of the Apostles and the Epistles, part II focuses only on the healing texts found within the Gospel accounts. The Gospel healing narratives are varied and numerous; in order to provide some limits on this project, I have chosen to deal only with those texts that are included in the Revised Common Lectionary. Most of the Gospel healing texts found in the new lectionary come from Mark, although there are three from Luke and one from John.

I have divided the texts into five separate chapters. Chapter 3 will deal with two texts about persons who are blind: the story of the man born blind, found in John 9:1-41 (Lent—Year A) and the story of Bartimaeus, found in Mark 10:46-52 (After Pentecost—Year B). Chapter 4 will focus on the *"Ephphatha"* text, in which Jesus heals a deaf man who has a speech impediment found in Mark 7:31-37 (After Pentecost—Year B). Chapter 5 analyzes the story of the paralyzed man, in Mark 2:1-12 (Epiphany—Year B). Chapter 6 deals with three texts that are related to ritual impurity: the healing of the leper, in Mark 1:40-45 (Epiphany—Year B); the healing of the ten lepers, found in Luke 17:11-19 (After Pentecost—Year C); and the healing of the woman with the flow of blood, found in Mark 5:25-34 (After Pentecost—Year B). Chapter 7 concludes part II with the story of the man from Gerasa who lived in the tombs: Luke 8:26-39 (After Pentecost—Year C). Although the man described in Luke 8:26-39 is still often referred to as "the Gerasene Demoniac," it is commonly assumed that the man lived with a form of mental illness.

Each chapter describes the disability of the person in the text as we know that disability today. Following this description is a section on the traditional hermeneutics scholars have used to study the text as well as current research from contemporary biblical scholars. In addition, I analyze how the text has been interpreted homiletically in this century and offer a critique as well as alternative suggestions for preaching the text based on a *healing* homiletic.

Before we proceed to the next chapter, a word is in order concerning my choice of terms to identify persons with disabilities. It is a difficult decision to make. I want to acknowledge people's right to name themselves with what-ever term is comfortable for them. While the common terms within society are "the handicapped" or "the disabled" or "persons with handicapping conditions," I have chosen not to use these. While "handicap" in horse racing or golf implies a leveling of the players so that an encumbrance is placed on the superior competitor, it has a different meaning for per-sons who are labeled "handicapped." Under the Elizabethan Poor Laws, persons with disabilities were granted permis-sion to be legal beggars—to place their caps in their hands in hopes of receiving alms. "The disabled" implies an ob-ject—a group possibly, but an object nonetheless—and says more about what the object cannot do than what it can.

In recent years, many other supposedly more liberating terms have emerged: physically challenged, differently abled, and so forth. I affirm these terms in their attempts to better identify the abilities of persons with limitations. These terms are widely used and often preferred by individuals and groups. Clergy with disabilities within my denomination have chosen the term "physically challenged" to identify themselves: The United Methodist Association of Physically Challenged Ministers. Unfortunately, on a societal level, these terms are often misunderstood. Because those in-volved with the writing of the new civil rights law for this country chose the term "Americans with Disabilities Act" (ADA) and because many who are working on a political level for disability rights have chosen to use the phrase "persons with disabilities," I have decided to use this term throughout the book as well.

The argument in favor of this phrase or any *one* phrase is that the proliferation of new vocabulary has divided the community rather than bringing it together under one umbrella for political and religious clout. The use of the term "persons with disabilities" for the International Decade of Persons with Disabilities and the ADA was an attempt to unify this tremendously diverse community under one banner.

In addition, I have accepted this term for myself. Because I have a hidden disability—one that is not apparent to others at most times—very few would identify me as a "handicapped" person or even as someone who is "differently abled" or "physically challenged." And yet I cannot deny the fact that I have a dysfunction within my body that limits me in a wide variety of ways. Recognition of my disability and the common experiences I share with others in the community contributes to a sense of connectedness. Identifying with and participating in the struggles of the community are important, but my disability is not the totality of who I am. I am first and foremost a person; hence I am a "*person* with a disability." Second, one aspect of who I am that cannot be denied by myself or by my friends, is that I have a disability; hence, I am a "person *with* a disability."

In respect to those with particular disabilities, I will always name the person first and then the disability that the person lives with: man who is blind, boy with epilepsy. Terms such as "epileptic," "demoniac," and "blind man" identify the person *as* their disability, rather than identifying their disability as one part of the person's life.

# PART I

## CHAPTER ONE

# Healing and Theodicy

---

One of the most difficult questions pastors and theologians have had to deal with throughout the ages is why there is so much suffering in the world. Volumes have been written in response to this question. Rabbi Harold Kushner tried to deal with this issue in his popular book *When Bad Things Happen to Good People*. This underlying question plagues many clergy today as they attempt to provide pastoral care to persons with disabilities—particularly those who are experiencing disability for the first time. A person has been in a car accident and wakes up in the hospital without the ability to walk. The long-awaited birth of a baby finally arrives, but joy turns to unknown fear as the expectant parents wait in silence while the doctors rush the newborn off to ascertain her physical condition. What do clergy have to offer to those who experience such suffering when the immediate shock and anger wear off and the questions are raised about why this happened to them? Where is God in the midst of their pain?

The questions are difficult. On the one hand, we have years of training, and many laity look to us for answers. For some people, clergy are the representatives of God, and they come to us not only for comfort but also for help in finding some meaning in their life situations. And while clergy may be exceptionally competent in many areas of ministry and feel in control of many situations, dealing with persons with disabilities makes many clergy uncomfortable. We have volumes to say on most topics (after all, preaching is a major part of our job), but we are uncomfortably silent when it comes to this particular group of people. We do not know what to say, we do not have any real answers, and their vulnerability raises in us questions about our own finitude and fragility. If this happened to them, what prevents me from being in their situation tomorrow?

In our attempts to deal with these issues and answer these questions, clergy have rightly relied on theology, tradition, and biblical guidance. The problem, however, is that Christian tradition and the Bible itself are very ambiguous on this topic, and clergy end up conveying mixed and often confusing, contradictory messages—in pastoral care settings and in preaching.

## Angel or Devil, Blessed or Cursed

One contradictory message many churches convey is that persons with disabilities are both blessed by God and cursed by God. Some within the Christian tradition label the persons with a disability as "angel" while others label the same person as "devil."[1]

Religious communities often view persons with disabilities as blessed, specially chosen by God to be courageous witnesses to the world. How often have we heard persons with disabilities praised for their perseverance, their inner strength, their visible witness that nothing in life will destroy their inner spirit or their will to make meaning out of their lives? Children with disabilities are often called "little angels." And parents with disabled children are seen as saints because of the "extra burden" they carry. We use words such as "valiant battle," "courageous woman," and "blessed by God," as we stand in awe at the ways some people are able to manage their lives, and we wonder if we would do as well.

Persons with disabilities are also considered blessed because the Bible implies that people have disabilities so that God's mighty works can be made manifest in and through them. They are blessed by God and used as witnesses to God's power. In 2 Corinthians 12:9 Paul says, "I will boast all the more gladly of my weaknesses, so that the power of Christ may dwell in me." Some believe that Paul's "thorn in the flesh" was some kind of disability. The writer of the Gospel of John credits Jesus with saying that the man "was born blind so that God's works might be revealed in him" (John 9:3). The parable in Luke about the great dinner indicates that it will be persons who are blind and lame who will taste the heavenly banquet, not those who were initially invited (Luke 14:16-24). Preachers have preached these texts in ways that continue to support the notion that persons with disabilities are blessed by God, and therefore are angels and saints.

At the same time, because of the literal and often traditional interpretation of many of the healing texts in the Gospels, persons with disabilities are often equated with the devil—they are perceived as being cursed by God. In recent years, a man who was born with severe physical deformities was looked upon with disgust and suspicion. Several times people said that only a pact with the devil could create such a grotesque being. They judged the man solely by his outward appearance. They found it difficult to imagine a God who would create such deformities. Therefore, they reasoned, the person with the disability must be of the devil.

Persons with disabilities are often considered sinful, lacking in faith, or even possessed by evil spirits or demons. The connection between sin and disease/disability that has emerged in the preaching of the healing texts has created a theological perspective that continues to permeate many of our churches today. Stories abound of persons with disabilities who have been told that if only they had enough faith, they would be cured.

Many people quote biblical sources to justify this position. Sin, or lack of faith, or demon possession must be the cause of disabilities, because in the story of the healing of the man who was paralyzed, "When Jesus saw their [the man's friends'] faith, he said to the paralytic, 'Son, your sins are forgiven'" (Mark 2:5). In Mark 5:34, in the story of the woman with the flow of blood who touched Jesus' cloak, Jesus says "Daughter, your faith has made you well." In Luke 9:39, it is an unclean spirit or demon that seizes the boy and "convulses him until he foams at the mouth."

Christian leaders and religious institutions explicitly or implicitly support these opposing images: blessed and cursed. Disability implies punishment for sin or lack of faith, but it also implies obedience to God's will in being a courageous witness to the world. What effect do these contradictory images have on the way persons with disabilities view themselves? How do these images affect how other people treat persons with disabilities in our churches and in society?

Both of these images—angel and devil, blessed and cursed—have a similar effect. Both cause other people to stay away and not become too involved. No one wants to become involved with someone who is cursed unless trying to convert or save that person. And most people see "angels" as a little too beyond their reality as they deal with the daily struggles of life. Whether they believe that persons with disabilities are blessed or cursed, the general belief is that their condition is God's will, and we should not interfere.

# God's Will

It is a basic human need to want to make sense out of times of struggle in our lives. It is difficult for people to believe that there is no purpose to their suffering. They want to know *why* this disability happened to them. For Christians, a common answer is that it must be God's will. We have been trained to believe that everything has a purpose in the larger divine plan.[2] *Why* it is God's will varies. There are many explanations that are traditionally given: (1) it is punishment for their sin or for the sin of their parents, (2) it is a test of their faith and character, (3) it is an opportunity for personal development or for the development of those in relationship to persons with disabilities, (4) it presents an opportunity for the power of God to be made manifest, (5) suffering is redemptive, and (6) the mysterious omnipotence of God simply makes it impossible to know why it is God's will.

## Punishment for Sin

This first rationale has already been dealt with in relationship to the perception of persons with disabilities as being cursed by God. There are many adult acts that we can label as sinful that might cause a disability—driving drunk and having a car accident, or destroying one's body and mind through drug use. In some cases it is easy for people to believe that God punishes adults for their sins. It is harder to believe that God punishes innocent children and infants for some sin they committed. Consider the story of Doug.

Doug's parents were a loving, successful couple. They tried for years to have a child. Finally, Doug was born. However, it was clear from the beginning that Doug had multiple disabilities. The extent of these disabilities would

23

be learned over the next few years. He was deaf and blind, he had to be tube-fed, he could not move his muscles very well. He died before his fifth birthday. What kind of God could intentionally make an innocent child such as Doug suffer in this way? What sin was he being punished for?

It was this same question that caused Augustine to resort to the concept of original sin. Augustine believed that all evil is the result of sin and its punishment, but he could not reconcile this belief with the suffering of innocent infants. Augustine's explanation, which is still very prominent today, was that all evil is a punishment for Adam's sin. Original sin became the sin of the race based on the fall of Adam. That was the only way Augustine could reconcile the suffering of infants with a loving God.

Today, Augustine's doctrine of original sin is insufficient as an explanation for a compassionate God who would cause some innocent children to be punished, as representatives of the human race, for the sin of Adam. Why should Doug be chosen to be punished for Adam's sin instead of some other child? But if we believe that God does not punish innocent infants, can we believe that God gives an adult a disability as punishment for sin? What about an eight-year-old or a fifteen-year-old? For what age-group is it appropriate to believe that the disability is caused by God as some form of punishment?

A variation on this belief is that the disability is God's punishment for the sin of one's parent or parents. Deuteronomy 5:9-10 is often quoted to justify this position: "You shall not bow down to them or worship them; for I the LORD your God am a jealous God, punishing children for the iniquity of parents, to the third and fourth generation of those who reject me, but showing steadfast love to the thousandth generation of those who love me and keep my commandments."

At a recent workshop, a clergywoman told me about her teenage daughter who was recently diagnosed as having a severe hearing loss. One day a woman who professed to be a Christian told this clergywoman that the reason her daughter was deaf was because the clergywoman had disobeyed God's laws by becoming an ordained woman. In this person's opinion, the daughter was being punished by God because her mother had decided to obey God's call to full-time ministry. For this woman, women ministers were clearly evil and deserved God's punishment, even if the punishment for this particular clergywoman was received indirectly through her daughter's disability.

Another form of this response occurs when infants suffer because of inherited or genetic disorders. Fetal alcohol syndrome, HIV (human immunodeficiency virus), and other birth defects are often caused by the actions of parents. Many people blame the parents for the suffering their children will experience through life, but few believe that God is punishing the children because of the parent's irresponsibility.

Even those who believe in the doctrine that disabilities are caused by God as punishment for sin recognize that this explanation does not reconcile some situations, such as Doug's, with our understanding of a loving God. When we look at the situation of children with disabilities, it becomes more difficult to believe that God gives a person a disability as some kind of punishment for sin. But people still seek answers for their question, "why me?"

## A Test of Faith

Another answer to the question "why me?" is that one's disability is God's will in order to test one's faith. In the case of Doug, people would admit that God probably was not testing an infant's faith; therefore, God must be testing his parents' faith. One is told that the disability is some kind of test from God and that if the test is "passed," the person will be stronger and more faithful because of it. What kind of test is it? How does one know if the test is passed or not? Traditionally, passing the test means being "healed"—that is, cured. But if the disability is still present, it is a sign that one's faith is insufficient.

This belief that God causes these disabilities in order to test our faith is fundamental to the practice of faith healing. If only persons with disabilities had enough faith, they would be "healed," which really means "cured." Disabilities are primarily the result of a lack of faith, and if the person would repent and believe "harder" or believe "more" or believe "deeper," he or she would be cured. Basically then, disabilities are a result of one's own arrogance and resistance to giving oneself over totally to God. And if the disability is permanent or some kind of chronic illness rather than a temporary one, it is clear that the person has not repented or has an inadequate and weak faith.

This is not to deny that "miraculous" cures may happen for some people because of medical science or even in spite of it. There are many things in this world that cannot be explained by any kind of science—medical or otherwise. Our bodies, minds, and spirits comprise an exceptionally complicated, integrated whole, and one can influence the others. The problem, however, is that there are some disabilities, such as an amputated leg, that cannot be "cured" no matter how faithful one is. There are also many good, faithful people who seem to endure much, while others who seem to be faithless are very healthy. To believe that disability is caused by God as a test of one's faith entails many inconsistencies. But there must be some explanation for disability that makes sense and can be reconciled with a loving, just God.

## Opportunity for Character Development

As people struggle to make sense of disability in relation-ship to God, another rationale emerges: disability provides an opportunity for personal growth and character develop-ment by overcoming obstacles. There are challenges for us to overcome and lessons for us to learn that come from our experiences of having a disability. The perseverance, coura-geousness, patience, and inner strength that label persons with disabilities as "blessed" rather than "cursed" are under-stood as part of the lessons that need to be learned by persons living with disabilities. What lesson God intends for each individual is not exactly known. Some struggle a lifetime to ascertain what it might be. This is not to say that persons with disabilities do not learn many things. Some of one's personal growth comes *because* of the disability and some *in spite of* it. But that is different from believing God *caused* a disability in order that one might learn a lesson or two. It is difficult to believe that any lesson could be learned by a baby who is born brain-damaged or by an older man when demen-tia has taken control of his life. And we wonder whether in some situations the amount of suffering and pain a person has to experience throughout life is worth whatever lesson is supposed to be learned.

Some would argue that what matters is not necessarily something that the person with the disability learns, but rather what the person contributes to society because of what doctors, psychologists, educators, and caretakers learn from the person. It is possible that God willed these disabili-ties to exist so that *others* can learn something from the ones with the disabilities. The research and testing done on many persons with rare disabilities enhances what medical science knows, and that knowledge may lead to a cure in the future. Psychologists and psychiatrists probe the minds of those

27

with mental illnesses to learn more about their own fields. A teacher develops patience and learns visual ways of experiencing the world when a deaf student is in the class. But is it right to use people as object lessons for our own personal growth? Can we believe in a God who intentionally causes someone to be paralyzed just so that another can learn a lesson?

Some contemporary "new age" concepts also support this notion that there is a lesson to be learned from disability. The difference is that instead of God deciding before or after birth that we have a particular lesson to learn, the person/soul makes its own decision (or decides in consultation with the divine) to be born disabled in order to learn a particular lesson. This resonates as well with Eastern religions that believe in karma and reincarnation. If we have all *chosen* the life we have in order to learn some lesson needed for spiritual growth, then persons with disabilities have no right to be upset about their situations. They chose the disabilities, whether they are currently conscious of it or not.

Whether decided by God or by the individual's soul before birth or by some combination of the two, the notion remains the same: for personal and spiritual growth, there are lessons to be learned, and this disability is the only or the primary mode by which one can learn them. It is true that persons with disabilities, like others, learn a wide variety of things throughout the various experiences of life. One learns many things because of the disability and many more lessons that have nothing to do with the disability. However, just because some lessons may not have been learned as quickly without the disability does not mean that God caused the disability for this purpose. Can any lesson be worth the frustration, the isolation, and in many cases, the agony and suffering that many people with disabilities experience?

## Manifestation of the Power of God

Some believe that people have disabilities, not for the purpose of learning or teaching lessons, but rather simply to show the power of God. Paul's boasting of his weaknesses so that Christ's power may dwell in him (2 Cor. 12:9) and Jesus' answer to the disciples that it was not the man's sin nor his parents' that caused his blindness but that the man "was born blind so that God's works might be revealed in him" (John 9:3) are scriptural basis for this belief. This doctrine implies that our purpose on earth is not about our worth as human beings, our own personal growth, or the contributions we can make to one another or to society as a whole. We are created so that God's works can be seen through us. But God's works are manifest in all creatures, not just those with disabilities. So why is disability uniquely related to God's power?

The "power of God" or "God's mighty works" is understood to be manifested primarily through miracles of faith healing. It is these miracles that convey the ultimate of God's power in Jesus' time and today as well. Persons with disabilities provide the opportunity for faith healing and miracles to take place. In order for a miracle to happen, there has to be an occasion where something "needs fixing." The person with the disability becomes an example of something that is "evil" and "needs fixing" and the miracle (i.e., cure) reveals God's power over such evil in the world. When "cures" are the primary mode by which persons can manifest the power of God, persons with disabilities are used as objects, often object lessons.

In situations like this, it is often not the faith of the person with the disability that is praised as contributing to the "cure," but rather the faith and charisma of the so-called "healer" that is lifted up as the mediator of the power of God.

The difficulty with this doctrine is that there are millions of persons in our world today who do not experience miracles, who are not cured of their disabilities. Some persons with disabilities die in institutions, abandoned by the church and sometimes by their families as well. They suffer for years alone. Katherine was born with multiple disabilities and was abandoned by her parents, who simply could not deal with the stress that her existence brought into their marriage. Katherine was lucky, however. She was adopted by a woman who gave her the care and love that she needed. But she died before the age of seven. What do we say when faith healing does not work? How can situations like this manifest the mighty works of God?

## Redemptive Suffering

The concept of redemptive suffering joins human suffering with the suffering of Jesus. Traditional Christian doctrine believes that we are saved through Christ's suffering. Because Jesus suffered for us on the cross and redeemed us from our sins, those Christians who suffer in the world today participate in the suffering of Jesus. Suffering in and of itself, then, is somehow redemptive, because those who suffer become more "like Jesus." The more one suffers on earth, the more Christlike that person becomes. Persons with disabilities who suffer through life because of physical, emotional, or mental illnesses and limitations are closer spiritually to the divine will because of their situation. They are redeemed through their suffering.

This concept is associated with the belief that persons with disabilities are specially chosen or blessed by God. The beatitudes are cited in support of this notion:

"Blessed are you who are poor, for yours is the kingdom of
    God.
"Blessed are you who are hungry now, for you will be filled.

"Blessed are you who weep now, for you will laugh.

"Blessed are you when people hate you, and when they
  exclude you, revile you, and defame you on account of the
  Son of Man. Rejoice in that day and leap for joy, for surely
  your reward is great in heaven; for that is what their
  ancestors did to the prophets.

"But woe to you who are rich, for you have received your
  consolation.

"Woe to you who are full now, for you will be hungry.

"Woe to you who are laughing now, for you will mourn and
  weep." (Luke 6:20-25)

The more one suffers, the more blessed one is and the greater
one's reward will be in heaven. While the "Blessed are you
. . ." texts are preached frequently, verses 24-25 are not
stressed as strongly or preached as often, since they require
a judgment on the powerful that says the reverse is also true.
If a person does not suffer, he or she is cursed. By ignoring
the "woe to you . . ." verses and focusing only on the "blessed
are you . . ." verses, the doctrine of redemptive suffering
becomes a judgment on the powerless and a rationale for
injustice. This doctrine is used not only for persons with
disabilities but also for those who are poor, hungry, and
homeless. It provides a future, heavenly reward so that
oppression of some by others can continue on earth.

When we look at so much poverty and homelessness in
our world, it is hard for us to believe in a God who would
cause so much suffering in exchange for a reward in heaven.
Besides, traditional Christian theology does not support a
heaven where some have a "more blessed" life than others.
Heaven is heaven—where all will be united with God.

It is true that blessings and transformations in one's life
can come through suffering, but that is the grace of God. It
is not the case that we must suffer in order to be redeemed.
The traditional doctrine of the atonement says that Jesus has

already done that for us. Suffering is not an end in itself. God's love was able to transform the crucifixion into a resurrection experience, but that is different from saying that God *caused* the crucifixion in order for there to *be* a resurrection.

The same is true for persons who suffer today. God's love is present in the midst of our pains and frustrations and can redeem those times in our lives, but God does not cause them to happen just so that we can suffer and therefore be more Christlike. Suffering in and of itself is not necessarily redemptive.

## God's Mysterious Omnipotence

When all other rational explanations fail, appeal is made to God's mysterious omnipotence. Human beings simply cannot understand why God does what God does, yet we still firmly believe that things are the way they are because God wills it. God's ways are not our ways, but there must be some purpose for disability in the grand scheme of life designed by God. God is omnipotent, but clearly God is also mysterious. We will never fully know, "why me." It is difficult for people to let go of the belief that God is somehow in control of this universe at every step of the way. Life seems too chaotic as it is. People need some assurance of a great puppeteer, or at least a grand design that in some future time and place will all make sense to us. We do not understand, but our not understanding and our affirming God's mysterious omnipotence also takes the responsibility away from us to do much about it. If it is God's mysterious will, we should simply let it be.

It is clear that attributing disability to God's will, no matter what rationale is given, conveys theological inconsistencies and mixed messages to our congregations in general and to persons with disabilities and their loved ones in particular. Punishment for sin is accepted for persons who have AIDS (acquired immune deficiency syndrome) but not for an infant born with Fragile X syndrome. We believe a person can fall and break a knee and be in a wheelchair for a few months in order to learn patience, how to slow down, and even sympathy for those who use a wheelchair every day of their lives, but the same rationale is usually not applied to a man in his seventies who has Alzheimer's disease. Faith healing is applied to those for whom a cure should be possible, but not to someone born without arms. We distinguish between adults and children, between those who are temporarily disabled and those with permanent disabilities, and between those whose disabilities are compensated by modern technology and those for whom daily existence is a struggle.

All of these answers are an attempt to make sense of often senseless situations while at the same time trying to maintain faith in God. But do these doctrines affirm belief in a God who is loving and wills the well-being of all of creation or in a God who is distant, erratic, and manipulative?

These explanations as to why disabilities must be part of God's will force parents, family members and persons with disabilities themselves to struggle deeply with belief in a loving God who would do such a thing to anyone. In difficult times, when faith and hope are needed, these doctrines place stumbling blocks in front of people. If the same scenario was played out in a movie, the person or thing that had so much control over people's lives and caused so much suffering and pain in the world would be considered a monster, not God. Where is the gospel, the good news for persons with disabilities? How can we reconcile a loving, nurturing, comforting God with a God who intentionally inflicts pain and suffering on certain members of the world's community?

# A Theology of Interdependence

As we examine our experiences as well as our church traditions and utilize our reason as well as Scripture, what would an adequate theology be for our time? If disabilities are not caused by God, what can we as communities of faith believe that reconciles the reality of disability with our faith in a loving, compassionate God?

To begin with, the notion of an all-powerful God needs to be redefined. For some, "all-powerful" or omnipotent means that everything that happens in the world is under God's control. God is indeed the great puppeteer. Natural disasters as well as personal crises are determined by God—or at least God has chosen not to stop them. It places God in the position of being responsible for nuclear accidents, wars, rape, the hole in the ozone layer, homelessness, famine, toxic waste dumps, and earthquakes, as well as disability. People need to believe that someone or something is in control of this world. God's power becomes more important than God's love and compassion.

But God is not a great puppeteer, and the choices that humans make are often responsible for the situations we are in. We are all interconnected and interdependent upon one another so that what we do affects the lives of others and the earth itself. All matter is interrelated. A person's DNA is directly related to her or his parents' genes and their parents' genes, and sometimes the combinations create the condition where disability will be the result. Sometimes matter is affected by other matter and mutations occur. Cancer and HIV are living organisms that are vying for control in the context of other living organisms. Everything in the universe is interconnected. All of life is interdependent. This is very clear in the global universe in which we live.

But in the midst of it all, we are confident that God wills our well-being. The Christian tradition is one of resurrection. In the midst of suffering and even death, God can bring about transformation. Well-being, however, is different for each person. What one considers devastating and tragic may not be so at all for another. We tend to place our values of well-being onto others. In the case of persons with disabilities, each person's situation is so very different that it is difficult to know the transformations possible for individual circumstances, but God knows.

I use the image of death and resurrection cautiously, because many persons with a disability do not equate their existential reality with suffering, let alone with death. What may seem atrocious to some people may not carry any of those same connotations for the person who has learned quite well how to live fully with his or her condition.

Deaf parents are often elated when their child is born deaf. Language and communication flows so much easier. The deaf child will grow up in the rich Deaf Culture, fluent in sign language, which will be the foundation for learning other languages such as English. Life is good, and except for discrimination from the outside world, there is virtually no suffering connected with being deaf. If a deaf child is born to hearing parents, however, it can be devastating for both the parents and the child as they attempt to grow together when the language of the parents is not easily transmitted to the child. Communication can be extremely difficult and tension-filled. For someone born without legs, needing to use a wheelchair to get around may be a nuisance, but it is "normal." However, for a marathon runner who has a car accident and emerges paralyzed from the neck down, the disability, at least initially, feels like a death—a tremendous loss. But whether one is dealing with prejudice and ignorance from the surrounding society or dealing with total dependence on machines and attendant care for survival, there is a word of hope and grace. God works to transform our lives at every moment, in all our various circumstances, through the power of love. God wills the well-being that is possible for each one of us.

These transformations are not necessarily the kind that we recognize as miraculous, although some clearly are. The possibility of transformation is present at every moment of our lives. Transformations for our well-being are present in ways that we are often not able to honor. When we think of a person who is deaf and blind, our minds conjure up the image of someone so deprived that their lives must exist in a permanently disvalued state, full of suffering and loneliness. They cannot see the wisps of clouds in the sky or the perfection of a rosebud opening to the sun; they cannot hear the ripple of a brook or a child's giggle. But who is to say that we are not missing just as much because we are not aware of the subtle nuances in the vibrations felt during a Mozart symphony, or the direction we are walking based on which side of our body is sunward and which is in the cool of the shadows, or the depths of emotion evoked by the feel of the bronze, the curve of the cut, and the depths of the grooves that etch an expression in the face of a sculpture. And the flutter of the heart when a loved one's presence is sensed is the same whether his footsteps are heard on the walkway or her face is glimpsed through the front window or his cologne is smelled in the brush of air as the door closes. God takes the lives that we have and provides transforming opportunities for us as we strive toward well-being.

I still remember the joy of accomplishment that Robbie had when he was convinced he had taught me how to roller-skate. Robbie had adrenoleukodystrophy, and though his eyes and ears were not damaged, the nerves coming back from his brain could not respond to the signals from his eyes and ears. So within a few weeks' time, at the age of six, Robbie became totally deaf and blind. He loved to roller-skate, so I would take him outside to a park with paved paths. I would just stand there and watch him as he created elaborate scenes in his mind. In his vivid imagination I, too, was on roller skates, but unlike him, I was a total novice. "Go straight . . . slow down! Watch out for the grass . . . here, hold my hand . . . better . . . better . . . straighten your back . . . okay now . . . turn . . . slowly . . . arms out for balance . . . good. You did it! Gee, I must be a great teacher!" He was so proud of himself at that moment. But people walking by would say, "How absolutely tragic," "The kid's crazy; don't let him make a scene like that." If he had been an adult, chances are that people would have wanted him to be put someplace away from the public. But Robbie was having a great time (and only once during the year I worked with him did he ask me, "Who turned out the lights?"). God was there through every debilitating progression of the disease to bring transforming moments of well-being into his life, and when Robbie died two years later, I believe he was transformed once again.

Devastations, sufferings, frustrations, and disabilities happen in this world. God does not cause them, but God is present in their midst to uphold us and transform us. Resurrection can happen in our lives without God causing the suffering and death *in order for* the resurrection to occur. God's grace is all-powerful and can turn pain into healing.

But how is this possible if God is not the great puppeteer? It is possible because the universe is interdependent, and God is a part of this interdependence. We experience the presence of God through someone's comforting touch, through the loving acceptance of another, through a hug or an invitation to table fellowship. Through faithful communion with others—true community—we experience the loving presence of God. We are agents of God in bringing about trans-formation in the lives of others. We work interdependently with God to achieve well-being for ourselves and others.

In the Christian community we use words such as "family of God," "communion of the saints," and "Body of Christ." This is the foundation of our faith, which identifies us as a people who are interdependent upon one another and upon God. We take care of one another, not only in times of crisis, but on a regular basis as well: a hand to hold before undergoing surgery, food for family and guests when a loved one has died, a ride to church for those who cannot or choose not to drive. The church as the family of God is there for all its members and for the world as well.

We are given no biblical or experiential reason to believe that life will be without any problems or crises or heartache. The biblical witness and the witness of the prophets and saints throughout history proclaim the presence of suffering. After Jesus preached his first sermon in the temple, "all in the synagogue were filled with rage. They got up, drove him out of the town, and led him to the brow of the hill on which their town was built, so that they might hurl him off the cliff" (Luke 4:28-29). And Paul says, "Three times I was beaten with rods. Once I received a stoning. Three times I was shipwrecked; for a night and a day I was adrift at sea" (2 Cor. 11:25). God did not cause these events or prevent them from happening, but God was there in the midst of them, offering strength and the possibility of transformation. The community of believers and the love of God supports us in our trials. "If one member suffers, all suffer together with it; if one member is honored, all rejoice together with it" (1 Cor. 12:26). Our Christian tradition is based on community and on our interdependence upon God and one another.

And yet our churches exist within the context of the American culture, which places a very high value on independence. We are shaped in part by the cultural message that we must pull ourselves up by our own bootstraps. These and like messages shape public opinion, encouraging the notion of independence as something toward which we must strive. Dependence is seen as something to be avoided. To be dependent is to be weak. It is tolerable for children and those in the last years of life to be weak and dependent, but for anyone between the ages of eighteen and seventy, dependence is suspect. Many persons with disabilities fall within this category.

The reality is that most persons with disabilities are dependent upon someone or something at various times in their lives. Deaf persons are often dependent on sign language or oral interpreters. Persons who are blind may be dependent on a Seeing Eye dog or a cane. Persons with mobility difficulties are dependent on walkers or crutches or wheelchairs, as well as ramps or elevators in multilevel buildings. Some people are dependent on medication, while others are dependent on persons within the medical profession for osteopathic or chiropractic manipulations, or for psychiatric help. Some persons are dependent on attendants to bathe and feed them, while others are dependent on accessible transportation in order to get to work. As technology increases, people who are unable to speak clearly are dependent on computers to talk for them.

But there is another kind of dependency. For many persons who live with a disability, the dependency on someone else or on something is the greatest determining factor for their quality of life and well-being. For others, it is often dependence upon body or mind that makes life so difficult. The inconsistency of one's ability to function either physically or mentally can make life seem unstable. It is hard to make plans without knowing whether one's body or mind will be functioning adequately enough so that the plans can be carried out. Dependency tends to foster a sense of dualism between one's mind and body. Most people do not have to worry about not being able to depend on their own bodies or minds for daily activities.

This dependency is difficult for other people to deal with as well. One minute the person with the disability may be functioning fine, but the next minute they may be incapacitated in some way. People can adjust their behavior patterns with persons with disabilities when they know what is appropriate and what is not at any given time. But when a person with a disability's needs change on a regular basis, that inconsistency also takes its toll on everyone else.

Dependency is tolerated if it is temporary. Someone has a gall bladder operation or comes down with pneumonia and people are there to help out with food and transportation. The community is present in this time of dependency. But it is different for someone who is dependent on a more permanent basis. The more severe the dependency, the less the person's presence is wanted within the community.

It is often this dependency that is frowned upon by society. Accessible transportation, sign language interpreters, elevators, and mental health centers cost money. The assumption is that the person with the disability does not contribute enough to society to make these services cost effective. The American motto of independence says that persons should be able to take care of themselves and not have to depend on society for basic survival and quality of life. In the life of the church, one's contribution is also balanced with cost. Sign language interpreters, assistive listening systems, braille hymnals, ramps and elevators all cost money.

The tendency is to talk about ministries *to* persons who are deaf or blind or using a wheelchair, with the underlying assumption that they are dependent upon the church and offer nothing in return. In some churches the language is changing to "ministry *with*," but there are still assumptions that it is really a one-way street rather than truly equal collaboration. The perspective is that persons with disabilities are dependent upon independent individuals. But an interconnected view of life recognizes that no one is totally independent. We are all interconnected and depend on one another and the created world for survival. Who we are influences who others are, and vice versa. As preachers, what we think strongly influences what others think. We are shaped both positively and negatively by those around us. We do not live in a vacuum. The negative attitudes society has toward adults who are perceived as weak and dependent greatly influence the lives of persons with disabilities. We know that one's self-esteem is shaped in large part by the support, acceptance, and respect one receives growing up. But when one's very existence is unacceptable to society at large, tremendous alienation and isolation can result.

The church, however, is called to be the place where people can be accepted for who they are as children of God, the place where dependency is acknowledged and interdependency is valued. Unfortunately, few of our churches are accessible, let alone welcoming and affirming of persons with disabilities. Yet,

> there are many members, yet one body. The eye cannot say to the hand, "I have no need of you," nor again the head to the feet, "I have no need of you." On the contrary, the members of the body that seem to be weaker are indispensable, and those members of the body that we think less honorable we clothe with greater honor, and our less respectable members are treated with greater respect; whereas our more respectable members do not need this. But God has so arranged the body, giving the greater honor to the inferior member, that there may be no dissension within the body, but the members may have the same care for one another. (1 Cor. 12:20-25)

41

The members of the body that *seem* to be weaker are indispensable, and God has so arranged the body, the community of believers, that the members may have the same care for one another. It is this interdependency in the midst of a culture that highly values independence that sets us apart.

A theology of interdependence honors the value of all individuals, not by what they do, but by who they are, recognizing that each and every person contributes to the community by being, not by doing. Interdependence acknowledges not only our dependence on God and one another, but also God's dependence on us to be agents of God's healing compassion in the world. It recognizes that all living organisms in the universe are connected and vying for life. Some of these have negative effects on others, and that is the reality in which we live. Disability happens; sometimes at conception from genetic factors, sometimes as a result of a difficult birth or improper health care in premature births, sometimes by a virus or cancer that is spreading through the body. Disabilities are also caused by environmental factors, and by the neglect or poor judgment of human beings through wars and accidents.

Disability is a part of everyday existence for millions of people and their loved ones in this world. Does God cause it to happen? No. That does not mean, however, that God is not present for us in the midst of it, willing each person's well-being even in the situation of permanent disability. The power of the resurrection image is that God can transform our lives through the healing touch of an interdependent community of faith.

When cure is not currently possible, healing can happen through the supportive, accepting community; through our own ability (undergirded by God's strength and the support of others) to make it through the hard times; and through the different, new possibilities that are open for us.

CHAPTER TWO

# Hermeneutical Hazards

One's theology about God clearly has a strong influence on one's interpretation of the healing narratives for homiletics. However, one's understanding of the Bible is equally important. If one believes in a literal interpretation of the Bible, the text is taken from its first-century context and applied directly to people today. This approach is based on firm belief in the truth of the miracle in the healing narratives and tends to focus on the faith or lack of faith of the person with the disability and the physical cure.

At the other end of the spectrum are those who believe that the Bible is a compilation of writings about a people's faith, much of which was composed by the writers themselves and not necessarily an account of what actually happened. Some preachers from this theological perspective do not believe in miracles and avoid preaching the healing texts altogether. Others try to explain the healings scientifically, and still others leave miracles in the realm of mystery and unexplained phenomena.

Most preachers from mainline denominations, however, are in between these two perspectives. They do not believe in the literal interpretation of the Bible and are not willing to make a commitment to faith healing and contemporary miracles, yet they also do not want to deny the possibility of miracles, the effect of sin on one's life, or the importance of faith. Their approach to the healing narratives is to preach these texts metaphorically. Metaphorical interpretations identify the disability of a few with the sins of many: for example, "We are all *deaf* to the word of God."

Both literal and metaphorical interpretations result in identifying the person with the disability in the text with sin in some way. On the one hand, the person either is being punished for sin or is lacking in faith; on the other hand, the physical reality of a few is equated with the disobedience and sin of many. Neither method treats the persons with disabilities in the texts as subjects in their own right. They are often used as objects or object lessons.

## *Bridging the Gap*

One of the most difficult tasks biblical preachers face today is understanding the text in its own context and then deciding what application (if any) the text has for today. The times we live in are so drastically different than they were two thousand years ago in the Hellenistic world that it becomes very difficult to deal with the Gospel healing texts. If someone were to encourage us to apply seventeenth- or even eighteenth-century medical concepts to diseases today, we would be appalled at the very notion, because of the enormous advancements science and technology have made since then. And yet we often unwittingly apply the medical worldview of biblical times to contemporary disability issues when we preach the healing narratives.

But we are not totally naive. Clearly, there are diseases today that were not in existence (to our knowledge) during Jesus' day, such as cancer and AIDS. We know that the causes of many diseases were not known, that genetics was not understood, and that the first-century worldview created other explanations for causes and cures of diseases and illnesses. Few preachers today would consider relating that medical worldview to contemporary diseases such as chicken pox, pneumonia, or cancer (although some preachers have declared AIDS to be the result of a person's sin). But disabilities such as deafness, blindness, and paralysis are different, because they are found in the biblical texts. Many ministers preach on the Gospel healing narratives and apply a first-century medical perspective to persons who are blind, deaf, or paralyzed now. The focus is more on cure than on healing. We preach the "demon possession" texts and attempt to apply biblical notions of demons to persons and issues today. Many of us intentionally or unintentionally apply first-century understandings of the nature of illness to a postmodern congregation because of the "authority" of the biblical text.

We use blindness and deafness in ways that have nothing to do with persons today who are blind and deaf. We preach about faith and sin and healing, and apply a first-century worldview to persons with these disabilities today without really considering what effect this has on their lives. But, we argue, the rhetoric sounds good, it preaches well, and it is biblical. What harm can it do? It can have an effect that is the opposite of what a sermon on a healing text intends.

In order to avoid preaching these Gospel texts in ways that are oppressive instead of healing, it is important to understand, as much as is possible, the worldview of the first century in relationship to disability.

## Medical Values: Now and Then

The medical values held by most Euro-Americans in the United States today are very different from those held by the early Christian community that wrote and compiled the books of the Bible (although there are some subcultures in America whose medical values are more similar to those of the early Christians than are those of most Euro-Americans).

John J. Pilch identifies five differing positions in socio-medical values between the communally oriented, agriculture-based cultures of the first century and the individually oriented, technology-based cultures of the twentieth century.

| FIRST CENTURY | TWENTIETH CENTURY |
|---|---|
| 1. prefers being or being-in-becoming | prefers doing |
| 2. prefers collateral or lineal relationships | prefers individualism |
| 3. focus is on present time | focus is on the future |
| 4. humans are subject to nature | humans control nature |
| 5. human nature is a mixture of basically good and evil; evil is expected in this world | human nature is good or a mixture of good and evil[1] |

Based on these values, a definition of health would be very different from one culture to another. For first-century peoples, it was one's sense of *being* in the community that was most crucial, and illness or disability interfered with one's being within the community.

In our modern-day context, health could be defined as "the ability to perform [doing] those functions which allow the organism to maintain itself [individualism], all other things being equal, in the range of activity [doing] open to most other members of the species and which are conducive toward the maintenance of the species."[2]

Disability goes against all of the values listed in the twentieth century column above. It often limits one's ability to "do"; it usually creates some sense of dependency on something or someone, which limits one's sense of individualism; because of the inconsistencies of one's physical or mental state and because of limited job opportunities in many cases, one's temporal focus is more in the present moment than in the future; and disability proves that we are not masters over nature. In the biblical context, blindness or deafness did not limit a person's ability to *do* but rather limited one's ability to *be* in relationship with the community. In our contemporary context, the focus is usually on blindness or deafness limiting a person's ability to *do*—to drive a car and therefore be independent, or to talk on the telephone.

Understanding illness and health from these two very different value systems will enable us to create a more appropriate hermeneutical bridge between the two cultures and times.

## Sickness, Disease, and Illness

Sickness is the general term for disability used during the first century. A. Young defines it as "a *process* through which worrisome behavioral and biological signs, particularly ones originating in disease, are given socially recognizable meanings, i.e., they are made into symptoms and socially significant outcomes."[3]

We do not worry much about a little cold because we can usually continue with our daily schedule at work and at home in spite of it. It may be a nuisance, and we may go to bed earlier, but it does not interfere too much with our life. If we get a bad case of the flu, however, our body aches, work becomes difficult, taking care of children feels like an impossible task, and cooking meals seems overwhelming. We just want to rest. Suddenly the "worrisome behavioral and biological signs" take on meaning with "socially significant outcomes." How many days can I call in sick without losing vacation days or pay? Am I neglecting the family or housework? When the disease takes on meaning, it is sickness.

There are two ways to understand or explain sickness: disease and illness. Disease is a modern concept. It focuses on "the abnormalities in the structure and/or function of organ systems."[4] Disease deals solely with the abnormalities within a particular individual's body. Since disease affects only that person's body, and the treatment of the disease is likewise focused on the individual alone, it was not of concern to the biblical world.[5]

Illness, on the other hand, was of great concern to those in the biblical world. Illness "is a socially disvalued state in which many others besides the stricken individual are involved."[6] One's friends and family as well as the broader community are affected by one's illness.

The people of the biblical world were concerned about the community and the effect sickness had in relationship to the order and workings of the community. In order to protect itself, the community established laws, including the purity codes—restrictions about temple worship and boundary concerns for those considered impure or unclean.[7]

Exclusion from the temple involved both the issue of needing boundaries for protection and the issue of purity or holiness. Nothing could defile the temple. For these reasons, Leviticus 21:17-23 forbids persons with disabilities from making offerings or going near the altar:

Speak to Aaron and say: No one of your offspring throughout their generations who has a blemish may approach to offer the food of his God. For no one who has a blemish shall draw near, one who is blind or lame, or one who has a mutilated face or a limb too long, or one who has a broken foot or a broken hand, or a hunchback, or a dwarf, or a man with a blemish in his eyes or an itching disease or scabs or crushed testicles. No descendant of Aaron the priest who has a blemish shall come near to offer the LORD's offerings by fire; since he has a blemish, he shall not come near to offer the food of his God. He may eat the food of his God, of the most holy as well as of the holy. But he shall not come near the curtain or approach the altar, because he has a blemish, that he may not profane my sanctuaries; for I am the LORD; I sanctify them.

This text is still used by many churches and denominations who interpret the Bible literally as one of the rationales for not ordaining persons who are blind, lame, or dwarfed; but no one would consider forbidding ordination to someone who had a broken arm, a rash, or bad acne based on this text.

In biblical times, the specific disease was not of great concern, and the focus was not upon the particular person. The concern was for the community. The particularities of the illness were only of concern as they related to the workings of the community. Illnesses caused relationships to be disrupted, and therefore created a sense of alienation and isolation.

The New Testament understanding of illness has both positive and negative aspects in relationship to persons living with disabilities today. On the one hand, the notion of illness from biblical times carries with it a more holistic understanding of the person and the illness's effect on the interdependent community. While traditional Western medicine is still divided into specialized disciplines, there is a growing movement today toward a more holistic approach to health care. Instead of focusing primarily on a particular organism or system within an individual's body, or on the chemical imbalance in a person's brain, we are beginning to perceive the body as a composite of various systems that are all interrelated. We are also seeing how the person is affected by the support systems (or lack thereof) in his or her life. The biblical notion of illness that deals with the whole person in relationship to the entire community can be very appealing.

On the other hand, the biblical focus on the community's involvement did not encourage *support* for the person with the illness, but rather resulted in the person's *exclusion* from the community, so that misfortune, demons, and curses could be warded off. The community was concerned, not about the disease itself (which Western medicine tends to overemphasize), but about the socially disvalued state of the person. The community drew boundaries to ensure protection, not for the person who was ill, but for the rest of the community. So while we may want to affirm the role of the community in relationship to an individual's illness or disability, the biblical answer of exclusion is not appropriate today. Jesus crossed boundaries in order to reconcile the one excluded with the community. Yet exclusion because of one's disability has continued in our churches since biblical times.

## Cure and Healing

Then and now, there are still two basic approaches to managing illness: cure and healing. When preaching the healing narratives, homileticians often use these terms interchangeably or at least use the term "healing" when what they really mean is "cure." We proclaim that Bartimaeus was "healed," but we are really preaching the belief that Bartimaeus was "cured." Yet in the English language, these are two very different words. *Cure* is the elimination of at least the symptoms if not the disease itself. *Healing*, on the other hand, has many meanings attached to it. Consider the phrases "healing presence," "healing moment," and "healing service." Each of these images elicits a sense of peace and of well-being, but they do not imply cure. While a healing worship service may include hope and even prayer for a cure for a particular individual, the intent of the service is to bring some sense of well-being into the person's life, a sense of comfort, support, and peace. Linda is blind and will be physically blind for the rest of her life, but she can still experience much healing in the midst of her blindness.

John Pilch states that with high mortality rates and limited knowledge of the body and diseases, cures were relatively rare in biblical times. "Biblical ancestors did not expect pain to be eliminated; it could only be alleviated . . . healing was quite likely not expected to be 'lasting.' "[8] But healing did take place, because one aspect of healing entails finding some sense of meaning in the midst of one's situation, some sense of well-being in spite of the illness. Kleinman says that "healing of illness takes place always, infallibly, since everyone ultimately finds some meaning to the life situations. . . . "[9] In the Hellenistic era, medicine, miracles, and performance rituals were all utilized in response to the disease.

Today, when illness occurs in our own lives, our first impulse is to seek some kind of medical solution to the problem. However, in relationship to disability and the preaching of these texts, the miraculous solution is implicitly or explicitly applied. And when the miraculous solution is applied, it is almost always focused on cure rather than on healing.

But what happens when a community has held a "healing" service with the intent of curing someone? What happens when the people have prayed fervently and laid hands on a person, truly expecting a miraculous cure, and it does not happen? Often the congregation is disheartened, and sometimes it is disillusioned. But for people with disabilities—particularly disabilities that modern medicine cannot cure—disappointment and disillusionment is coupled with feelings of rejection. Insisting on a cure implies that the community does not accept them as they are but will fully accept them only if they become like everyone else. No matter how well-intentioned the community is, this can be a devastating experience for the person with a disability. If the cure does not happen, the person is left with the sense that he or she is unacceptable to the community.

Often, people simply want what is best for persons with disabilities; and since the best, in their minds, is physical "perfection" (i.e., a cure), they pray for a miracle. But "perfection" is determined by peoples' values. Our definition of physical perfection, what we believe is "best," or what we think is "healing" may not be the same for the person with the permanent disability. Sameness of physical ability and attribute should not be so valued that it devalues physical difference. When the disability is not accepted as part of who the person is, exclusion from the community is the result.

But Jesus' actions in the Gospel healing narratives resulted in the person with the disability being reintegrated into the community. "Jesus' therapeutic activity restores afflicted individuals to purity, to wholeness . . . restored to full and active membership in the holy community, the people of God."[10] Jesus broke down the social boundaries that were established by the society for protection. Instead of Jesus becoming contaminated by the lepers who were labeled unclean, the lepers were able to go back to their family and friends and to participate in temple worship. After living with a flow of blood for twelve years, alienated and isolated from any kind of relationship, the woman is welcomed back into the community—Jesus even calls her "daughter." The sick person is restored to an appropriate mode of *being*—not of *doing*. The breaking down of those barriers allowed the *being* of the person to be affirmed again and to experience healing.

While being-in-community was valued in first-century biblical culture, contemporary American culture values doing—being able to function well and thereby contributing something to society. And yet being-in-community is an appropriate image for healing in an interdependent Christian community. Healing happens when the well-being God offers is experienced. This may entail elimination or alleviation of the illness, but in the case of permanent disability, healing often happens in the midst of managing the disability rather than in any kind of "cure." The community participates with God in offering possibilities of well-being to one another.

Bridging the gap between the biblical world and our own can be difficult when preaching these Gospel healing narratives. But understanding common first-century beliefs about the cause of illness, the relationship illness has to *being* rather than *doing*, the concept of healing versus cure, and the notion of healing being interconnected with participation in the community, can assist us greatly as we negotiate this large gap. Preachers must struggle with their own beliefs about causes of illness, healing versus cure, and the relationship persons with disabilities have with the community.

Will the community be one that brings healing through acceptance, support, and encouragement, or will the community of faith establish boundaries to protect itself from those considered unclean or cursed? Will our preaching imply that one has to be physically and mentally "whole" (based on the preacher and congregation's definition of "wholeness") through miracle or medicine in order to be an active participant in the life of the church, or will difference be honored and accepted? Will our preaching nurture an interdependent community where we are agents of the daily miraculous transformations God wills for each of our lives?

## Metaphorical Interpretations

Another common way to approach the healing narratives is to preach these texts metaphorically. While the texts are stories about specific people in a particular time and place, the person with the disability in the text is often used by the Gospel writers as a representative for a larger group. Particularly in the Gospel of Mark, the disciples ask irrelevant questions, argue about things unimportant, and do not seem to grasp the significance of Jesus' ministry. For Mark then, these texts function both as stories of actual physical miracles and as symbolic constructs to emphasize the inability or refusal of the disciples to understand who Jesus was.[11] The disciples were "blind" and "deaf" in relationship to Jesus' purpose on earth.

Preachers who choose this metaphorical approach to preaching tend to identify the congregation as the contemporary disciples who are "deaf" to God's commands and "blind" to the saving grace of Jesus. There are several problems, however, in dealing with "blindness," "deafness," "paralysis," "muteness," or any other disability as metaphors.[12] The main problem in using these terms metaphorically in this way is that blindness, deafness, and paralysis are always used in negative ways in religious vocabulary. The metaphorical use of these terms is then identified with "refusal to understand" or "disobedience to God" or "refusal to act according to the will of God" and are therefore labeled as willful, selfish behaviors. Consider the following quotations:

You can be blind in a pew, and deaf in front of an altar. [13]

. . . the blindness of man who praises the miracle-worker . . . but wants nothing to do with his cross.[14]

People are too deaf to catch the sobs of grief . . . too hard of hearing, to catch the rumble of discontent over injustice.[15]

In short, using these terms metaphorically equates the sin of those who can see, hear, and move, with the physical reality of those who cannot. The result is that the words themselves carry with them a negative connotation, and deafness, blindness, and paralysis become equated with sin. The metaphorical usage is transferred onto those who live with these physical realities on a daily basis. The negative result may be somewhat softened by those preachers who clarify their metaphorical use of these terms by preceding them with the word "spiritual": as in "spiritual blindness" or "spiritual deafness." But for those who live with these physical realities, using blindness, deafness, and paralysis metaphorically continues to contribute to the negative, oppressive attitudes people have towards persons who are blind, deaf, or paralyzed. What we mean to communicate by these metaphors is a judgment against insensitivity and indifference or outright disobedience—not against deafness and blindness per se. The negative implications of sensory language become commonplace as its metaphorical use becomes accepted truth in homiletical discourse. Sensitivity to the way we use sensory language adds another dimension to the struggle for inclusive and emancipatory liturgical language.

By using these terms metaphorically, we also imply that blindness, deafness, and paralysis are *choices* people make: a person *chooses* not to see/understand, a person *chooses* not to hear/listen, and a person *chooses* not to move/act. But blindness, deafness, and paralysis are not choices made, but physical inabilities to see, hear, or move. The issue is not one of conscious decision or control. This contrasts strongly with the situation of sin these disabilities are mistakenly chosen to symbolize.

Persons with disabilities then, carry the double burden of those who preach these Gospel healing narratives from the perspective that if only their faith were strong enough, they would be cured, which implies that disability is a punishment for sin or for lack of faith; and those who preach these texts metaphorically, using blindness, deafness, and paralysis as analogies of sin. Either way, the liberating word of "healing" is fundamentally missing for persons with disabilities. By not negating the concept that disability is equated with sin, either literally or metaphorically, we as preachers continue to contribute to the alienation of persons with disabilities rather than reaching out and embracing them into a healing community of faith.

# PART II

# CHAPTER THREE

# Blindness

---

There are five different narratives of persons who are blind in the Gospels: (1) the two men who were blind, in Matthew 9:27-31; (2) a very brief mention of a man who was considered to be possessed by a demon and who was also blind and mute, in Matthew 12:22; (3) the man from Bethsaida who was blind, in Mark 8:22-26; (4) the story of the man who was blind (known in Mark as Bartimaeus) sitting by the road to Jericho, which is found in all three Synoptic Gospels (Matt. 20:30-34; Mark 10:46-52; Luke 18:35-43); and (5) the long narrative of the man born blind, in John 9:1-41. There are also several general references to Jesus giving sight to those who were blind. Mark's account of Bartimaeus's healing and John's story of the man born blind are the two texts that are included in the Revised Common Lectionary.

John's narrative is a story of controversy between Jesus and the Pharisees. The cure happens early in the story, and the remainder of the text deals with the Pharisees' attempt to ascertain who it was that cured someone on the sabbath and how it happened. The story builds to a confession from the man born blind that Jesus is the "Son of Man." In contrast, Mark's narrative deals with the condition and the actions of Bartimaeus that lead up to his cure—the climax of the story.

Homiletically, the blindness texts have so often been preached metaphorically that "blind" and "blindness" are the most common sensory terms in religious vocabulary. They are always used in a negative connotation; usually in reference to our refusal to obey or pay attention to what God wills for our lives. The presence of persons who are blind in our congregations and communities seems to go unnoticed as pastors consistently use "blind" and "blindness" as metaphors for living in some state of sin. These terms are also used to denote a "pre-Christian" state—a time before coming to know Jesus. This is made clear in the popular hymn "Amazing Grace": "I once was lost, but now am found; was blind, but now I see."

A friend of mine is an African American clergywoman who is also blind. She has consistently been fighting for the rights of persons with disabilities and has been on the cutting edge of justice issues—in terms of race, gender, and disability. I asked her one day what she did with the hymn "Amazing Grace" and the blindness phrase in that song. At the time she was pastoring a church in the Midwest. She replied, "I just stand up front and sing 'was blind and still can't see!'" We might argue that the phrase in the hymn is simply symbolic of one's relationship with God—that it is not intended to be literal. But it implies that once a person has faith, he or she will see again. It evokes the theological position that if people who are blind only had enough faith, they would regain their sight. But Christians who are blind still cannot see, and blindness is still equated with sin.

## Blindness

Most people assume that a person who is considered "blind" cannot see anything. That is not necessarily true. Certainly there are persons who are completely blind, but a person can be identified by the government as "legally blind" and still be able to perceive lightness and darkness, images that never come into focus but are shapes nonetheless.

Today, persons who are blind can do just about anything (with certain exceptions, such as driving a car or being a surgeon). This is not to deny that there are limitations that come with being blind or that persons who become blind later in life do not have a very difficult time adapting to their new reality. And certainly other factors can complicate the life of a person who is blind: lack of education or support systems, unemployment, poverty, other disabilities, poor self-esteem—all these issues that reduce anyone's possibilities of functioning well in the world. But there are so many programs and support services available today that persons who are blind in the United States can function very well.

Trust is one of the major issues that all persons who are blind face. People who are blind have no choice but to trust the people around them—not just friends and family, but complete strangers. They trust their coworkers not to move the furniture without telling them. Those who cannot see at all have to trust cashiers and bank tellers to give them the right amount of money—have to trust someone to tell them which bills are fives, which are ones, and which are tens. They trust someone to read onto tape the textbook required for a class—*before* the test is given. They trust the person who reads their mail to keep personal things confidential, and they trust someone to tell them when someone played a joke on them and stuck a tacky, plastic pink flamingo in their yard, with its wings turning in the wind! Trusting others is not an option. Relationships with others are crucial.

Another related issue is that of dependency on others—especially for transportation. In a city where public transportation is frequent and dependable (Is it even conceivable to put "public transportation," "frequent," and "dependable" in the same sentence?), persons who are blind can get around fairly well. In a more rural area, or in a city with inadequate public transportation, they need to depend on others for transportation. Most clergy would cringe at the idea of calling a parishioner for a ride every time they needed to make hospital or home visitations. But the clergy I know who are blind often find that getting a ride from a layperson fosters lay participation in hospital and home visitations, which empowers the laity and creates a stronger community ownership of the pastoral care ministry of the church. Like trusting, depending on others is a daily reality for many.

Transportation is not the only area where persons who are blind are dependent on others. It may be as simple as depending on someone to explain what is happening in the movie on TV when it is all action and no one is speaking, or depending on someone to help them shop for food amidst the cans and boxes that all feel alike, or depending on someone to help them match colors when shopping for clothes. Interdependency becomes an integral part of reality and a daily necessity.

With modern technology, millions of persons around the world are able to have their vision corrected with glasses or contact lenses. Operations can help some whose vision loss is more severe. But there are still millions of persons in the United States and even more around the world whose vision cannot be corrected. What does healing mean when cure does not seem possible? How have the two blindness texts that are in the lectionary been preached? What insights can be gained by looking at these texts from a disability perspective?

The Text
**John 9:1-41**

> ¹As he walked along, he saw a man blind from birth. ²His disciples asked him, "Rabbi, who sinned, this man or

60

his parents, that he was born blind?" [3]Jesus answered, "Neither this man nor his parents sinned; he was born blind so that God's works might be revealed in him. [4]We must work the works of him who sent me while it is day; night is coming when no one can work. [5]As long as I am in the world, I am the light of the world." [6]When he had said this, he spat on the ground and made mud with the saliva and spread the mud on the man's eyes, [7]saying to him, "Go, wash in the pool of Siloam" (which means Sent). Then he went and washed and came back able to see. [8]The neighbors and those who had seen him before as a beggar began to ask, "Is this not the man who used to sit and beg?" [9]Some were saying, "It is he." Others were saying, "No, but it is someone like him." He kept saying, "I am the man." [10]But they kept asking him, "Then how were your eyes opened?" [11]He answered, "The man called Jesus made mud, spread it on my eyes, and said to me, 'Go to Siloam and wash.' Then I went and washed and received my sight." [12]They said to him, "Where is he?" He said, "I do not know."

[13]They brought to the Pharisees the man who had formerly been blind. [14]Now it was a sabbath day when Jesus made the mud and opened his eyes. [15]Then the Pharisees also began to ask him how he had received his sight. He said to them,

"He put mud on my eyes. Then I washed, and now I see." [16]Some of the Pharisees said, "This man is not from God, for he does not observe the sabbath."But others said, "How can a man who is a sinner perform such signs?" And they were divided. [17]So they said again to the blind man, "What do you say about him? It was your eyes he opened." He said, "He is a prophet."

[18]The Jews did not believe that he had been blind and had received his sight until they called the parents of the man who had received his sight [19]and asked them, "Is this your son, who you say was born blind? How then does he now see?" [20]His parents answered, "We know that this is our son, and that he was born blind; [21]but we do not know how it is that now he sees, nor do we know who opened his eyes. Ask him; he is of age. He will speak for himself." [22]His parents said this because they were afraid of the Jews; for the Jews had already agreed that anyone who confessed Jesus to be the Messiah would be put out of the synagogue. [23]Therefore his parents said, "He is of age; ask him."

[24]So for the second time they called the man who had been blind, and they said to him, "Give glory to God! We know that this man is a sinner." [25]He answered, "I do not know whether he is a sinner. One

thing I do know, that though I was blind, now I see." [26]They said to him, "What did he do to you? How did he open your eyes?" [27]He answered them, "I have told you already, and you would not listen. Why do you want to hear it again? Do you also want to become his disciples?" [28]Then they reviled him, saying, "You are his disciple, but we are disciples of Moses. [29]We know that God has spoken to Moses, but as for this man, we do not know where he comes from." [30]The man answered, "Here is an astonishing thing! You do not know where he comes from, and yet he opened my eyes. [31]We know that God does not listen to sinners, but he does listen to one who worships him and obeys his will. [32]Never since the world began has it been heard that anyone opened the eyes of a person born blind. [33]If this man were not from God, he could do nothing." [34]They answered him, "You were born entirely in sins, and are you trying to teach us?" And they drove him out.

[35]Jesus heard that they had driven him out, and when he found him, he said, "Do you believe in the Son of Man?" [36]He answered, "And who is he, sir? Tell me, so that I may believe in him." [37]Jesus said to him, "You have seen him, and the one speaking with you is he." [38]He said, "Lord, I believe." And he worshiped him. [39]Jesus

said, "I came into this world for judgment so that those who do not see may see, and those who do see may become blind." [40]Some of the Pharisees near him heard this and said to him, "Surely we are not blind, are we?" [41]Jesus said to them, "If you were blind, you would not have sin. But now that you say, 'We see,' your sin remains."

# Hermeneutics

This is one of the most important texts in the Bible for those within the disability community. In this text John portrays a situation where the disciples ask Jesus who sinned, the man born blind or his parents? And Jesus responds: "Neither this man nor his parents sinned; he was born blind so that God's works might be revealed in him" (v. 3). This part of the response is often quoted as assurance from Jesus that disability is not punishment for anyone's sin.

This section however, is just one small part of a much longer pericope. It is a cleverly written drama full of many different elements. It is found in the ninth chapter of John, which is part of the "Book of Signs" section of the first half of this Gospel. The "Book of Signs" is the author's way of moving his audience beyond a fascination with the often spectacular deeds of Jesus to his true christological identity.

John's Gospel is different from the other Gospels in its description of miracles. There are elements in this particular text that are not found in any healing narrative in the Synoptic Gospels: (1) the man has been blind *from birth*;

(2) Jesus uses *mud* (not just saliva, as in Mark 7:31-37 and Mark 8:22-26) as part of the remedy to effect the cure; (3) the final cure takes place through the waters of *Siloam*; (4) the Pharisees *interrogate* the man born blind about the miracle; and (5) the Pharisees question the *parents* of the man who was blind.[1]

This text evolved into its current state. The oldest element is the healing story, which has three parts: "a description of the sickness, the act of healing, and some confirmation of the miracle."[2] The trial scene, in which the man is accused of being a follower of Jesus, is tried, and is driven out of the synagogue, was added later. John then added the christological elements (vv. 4-5), which declare Jesus to be the light of the world and include the discussion of his origins (vv. 29-34).[3]

This text is long and complicated, but it can be divided into seven sections: (1) Verses 1-7 focus on the question posed by the disciples, Jesus' answer, the administrations and command by Jesus to the man, the man's washing in the pool, and the cure. (2) Verses 8-12 concentrate on the man's return and the confusion of the neighbors as to his identity. In this section, the man identifies his healer as the *man* Jesus. (3) Verses 13-17 deal with the Pharisees' interrogation of the man concerning his previous state, his current state, and who effected the man's transformation from being blind to now being able to see. At the end of this section, the man identifies Jesus as a *prophet*. (4) Verses 18-23 describe the interrogation by the Pharisees of the man's parents. (5) Verses 24-34 continue the interrogation by the Pharisees about what happened and by whom. Jesus is accused of being a sinner, and the man is accused of being one of his followers and is driven out of the synagogue. (6) Verses 35-38 tell us that the man was alone, and Jesus heard of his being cast out of the synagogue and sought him out. Jesus reveals himself as the Son of Man, and at the end of this section, the man exclaims "Lord, I believe," and worships Jesus. (7) Verses 39-41 end the narrative with a final discussion between Jesus and the Pharisees.[4]

As Christianity was spreading, this text was utilized by John and his early Christian community as an apologetics in the growing debate over Jesus' true identity.[5] This is most obvious in the interrogation section of the narrative. The question is whether Jesus has divine power or not, and if he does, who is he? The text is an attempt to convince people of the divine nature of Jesus.

## Scene 1 (Verses 1-7)

*Verse 1:* In this verse we learn that the man was *born* blind. A recent homiletics lectionary resource equates the man's blindness with imperfection: "Notice that the man was born blind—meaning, *created imperfectly . . .* " (emphasis mine).[6] The author may be referring to a first-century belief that persons born with disabilities were "imperfect," but the statement implies that persons who are blind today are also imperfect, not whole.

But who is created perfectly? And who decides the definition of perfection? This kind of language contributes to the second class citizen (humanity?) status that many persons who are blind experience.

*Verse 2:* The question from the disciples about who sinned sets up the healing narrative section of the text. The notion that disability is caused by the sins of the parents has its roots in Exodus 20:5 and 34:7, which are quoted and reiterated in Numbers 14:18 and Deuteronomy 5:9. Some Jews believed in the preexistence of the souls and in the ability of these souls to sin in the womb.[7] The disciples' question asks Jesus to clarify these notions.

*Verse 3:* Jesus' response puts an end to the discussion by saying that the disability is not caused by anyone's sin. Yet the explanation Jesus gives for the disability is not exactly clear. He says, "he was born blind so that God's works might be revealed in him." But what exactly does this mean? One scholar says that the man had to be blind because "A whole man would have been of no use to Christ. . . . [I]t was his blindness, his cross as men say, that gave him his chance to be of such signal service to the Master."[8] This statement reiterates the opinion of the lectionary resource that the man was not *whole,* and identifies blindness as a "cross" given by God.

Another scholar interprets this verse very differently: "John thought it not untoward for God to have sent the poor man through years and years of life as a blind beggar so that one day he might, so to speak, serve as an object lesson. Why inflict him with years of blindness in the first place?"[9] Many in the disability community interpret this verse to mean that the man was born (like all of us) to show God's love to the world.

*Verses 4-5:* These are christological additions that portray Jesus as the light of the world. John's wordplay on day/light/seeing and night/darkness/blindness reiterates one of the running themes of this Gospel—the theme of light and darkness.

*Verse 6:* Much is implied in this verse that is not obvious. We have no idea if the man born blind overheard the conversation between Jesus and the disciples. Even if he did, he may have guessed the person was a teacher but not necessarily a healer. Unlike Bartimaeus, this man does not ask for mercy or to be healed. The man may have absolutely no idea what is happening to him. He cannot see what is going on. Then suddenly, with no warning, someone is putting mud on his eyes. Imagine being blind, not knowing what is happening around you, and then feeling dirty mud being smeared on your eyes. You would be shocked, confused, and probably scared. On the other hand, there is the notion that Jesus takes the initiative in reaching out to us, rather than waiting for us to cry out to him as in the case of Bartimaeus. This initiative of Jesus is not dependent on the faith of the man born blind. The man has no idea what is happening. The man's belief in Jesus comes long after the cure itself. The cure is not dependent on anything the man says or does. It is a gracious gift. But it also feels like the man is used as an object—an object lesson perhaps. Maybe the man would have preferred to be a joint participant in the decision rather than have the cure done *to* him.

*Verse 7:* Next, the person who has put mud on his eyes says to the man, "Go, wash in the pool of Siloam." Was someone playing a practical joke on him? Of course he wanted to wash the mud off as soon as possible. The pool may have been the closest water source where he could do this. We do not know. He may also have been trying to figure out exactly what was going on. He may have been familiar with the use of spittle-mud by common folk healers of the day. Arthur John Gossip portrays a rather pitiful picture of the man trying to find his way to the pool of Siloam: " . . . face daubed with dust and clay and spittle . . . tapping his way through the public streets . . . feeling himself no doubt a ridiculous spectacle."[10] While these images may be vivid, I believe this kind of language from the pulpit encourages people to look at persons who are blind today as those whose eyes are glazed over, tapping their way through the public streets with their canes, being a ridiculous spectacle among those in society who are born "perfect" instead of "imperfect."

When the man washed in the pool, he was able to see. The author of John, however, wants us to have additional information. We are told that the word Siloam means "Sent." Some scholars equate the healing powers of the waters of

"Sent" with the healing powers of Jesus, the one who is *sent*.[11] Fuller suggests that the pool of Siloam was also "known as illumination" and was connected with baptism.[12] This connection between the waters of Siloam, the movement from not seeing/understanding to seeing/believing, and the text's relationship to baptism in the early church will be examined in more depth in the section "A Healing Homiletic," below.

## Scene 2 (Verses 8-12)

*Verse 8:* Here it is confirmed for us what we suspected— the man born blind begged for a living. The connection between persons with disabilities and begging has been a constant throughout history. It contributes to a basic perception that persons who are blind are also poor, helpless, pitiful creatures. It is a difficult concept to overcome today in America. And in other places around the world, the truth is that begging is still the only means by which many persons with disabilities can stay alive. There are horror stories of adults abusing children by disabling them in a variety of ways so that they will be all the more pitiful and pitiable as they are sent to beg in the streets to earn their keep.

*Verses 9-10:* In these verses, the neighbors do not celebrate the transformation that has taken place in this man, but rather they argue over whether it is the same man or not and how this could have happened. The community is antagonistic rather than accepting.

*Verse 11:* Here it is clear for the first time that the man knows the name of his healer. This verse marks the beginning of the man's progression in recognizing who Jesus is. "The *man* called Jesus. . . . "

*Verse 12:* The neighbors want to know where this man Jesus is. But since Jesus disappears from the text at verse 7, we do not know if, upon his return from the pool of Siloam, the man saw Jesus face-to-face or if Jesus had already left. At this point, the man still may not know what Jesus looked like, since he had been blind at their first encounter.

## Scene 3 (Verses 13-17)

*Verse 13:* Clearly the people of the community do not believe the word of the man who was born blind. They bring him to the Pharisees, who should be able to explain what has happened.

*Verses 14-15:* Likewise, the Pharisees do not believe the man, and they too interrogate him about the healing—how and by whom it happened.

The word of a person who is blind today is still often not believed. In the courts, the testimony of a person who is blind is very suspect, because a person who is blind cannot possibly have "seen" the events in question. Because they cannot qualify as "eyewitnesses," people who are blind are highly questioned, and their word is often not believed. The testimony of people who are blind, regarding what they have smelled, felt, or heard has been accepted in some legal cases, but their word is still highly suspect.

*Verse 16:* Jesus is considered a sinner rather than one sent by God because he does not observe the Sabbath law.

*Verse 17:* Here, the man's understanding of who Jesus is has progressed from seeing Jesus as am an to seeing him as a prophet. "He is a *prophet*."

## Scene 4 (Verses 18-23)

*Verses 18-23:* Since the neighbors and the Pharisees do not believe what the man says, they call his parents in to testify for him. The text implies that the parents were uncooperative because they were afraid of being "put out of the synagogue." But they really did not know anything more than what their son told them. In verses 21 and 23, his parents comment "he is of age." He can speak for himself!

What the Pharisees did is very common today as well. Persons who are blind are often treated as children throughout their adult lives. Strangers will talk to the friends or family of a person who is blind, but are uncomfortable directly addressing the person who is blind. This implies that persons who are blind cannot speak for themselves or understand what is going on around them. While they are not deaf, there is a common misconception that they somehow need an interpreter in order to understand what is being said. In the deaf community it is even worse. People will talk to the interpreter rather than talking to the person who is deaf. Either way, the person with the disability becomes invisible—nonexistent.

Although the parents in the text may be motivated by a selfish concern, they at least treat their son as an adult, a subject in his own right. They believe he is able to speak for himself and to make his own decisions. They are not overprotective of him.

*Verse 22:* Excommunication from the synagogue of Jews who accepted Jesus as the Messiah did not begin until around A.D. 90, so the excommunication in this text was probably a later addition to this story, which supposedly took place during Jesus' lifetime.[13] This was an important issue for the author of John's Gospel, for he was writing to a community which was experiencing this rejection by the Jewish religious authorities for believing in Jesus.

# Scene 5 (Verses 24-34)

*Verses 24-26:* Again, the man is called before the Pharisees to explain what has happened to him.

*Verse 27:* The man's retort in this verse is both clever and arrogant. He speaks up boldly and says, "I have told you already, and you would not listen. Why do you want to hear it again? Do you also want to become his disciples?" The sarcastic tone of his last question implies that he is winning this argument with the Pharisees. He does not shrink in the face of judgment, insult, and oppression, but rather shows himself as one who is not afraid of those in authority and power. His strong wit, personality, intellect, and ability to communicate are not traits he developed *after* he was able to see. All of these were developed while he was blind, probably *because* he was blind.

Verses 28-29: The man born blind is negatively accused of being a disciple of the unknown Jesus while the Pharisees boast of being disciples of Moses.

*Verses 30-32:* In another verbal retort, the man argues with the Pharisees with language and doctrines familiar to them.

*Verse 33:* Indirectly, the man confesses that Jesus is not just a man, and not just a prophet, but is *from God.*

*Verse 34:* The man who was born blind is accused of being born in sin (which Jesus earlier contradicted), and he is judged harshly for trying to teach the Pharisees something. The Pharisees did not believe the word of the man born blind and they certainly are not about to listen to any teachings from a beggar. They are the religious leaders, wise and educated. What could they possibly learn from a poor beggar who has been blind all his life until now? This is the attitude many persons who are blind still face today. Society still has a hard time believing that they have anything to contribute to society, anything to teach those who are not blind. Teaching and service is too often assumed to be a one-way street: those who are blind are the passive recipients, not the active givers.

The result of the man's boldness and smart retort is that, although he is now able to see, he is still forbidden to be a part of the religious community. Here is a man who did not ask to be cured, but as a result of being cured he is cast out from the community. In other healing narratives, it is the presence of the disability that causes rejection by the religious community. The cure, then, allows the person to be integrated back into the community. In this story, however, the cure results in the man's being excluded rather than reintegrated. Being able to see does not necessarily make his life easier or happier.

Today, persons who are blind and those with other disabilities are speaking up boldly in both the church and society in an attempt to claim their equal place in the community. Some are demanding their rights to access in education, employment, and church services. And like the man in this text, when they are bold and speak up for themselves, they are seen as being too pushy or aggressive, rather than as the passive receivers they are expected to be. They too experience rejection by faith communities.

## Scene 6 (Verses 35-38)

*Verse 35:* Jesus has been absent from the scene since the man received his sight. But here we are told that Jesus hears of the man's being driven from the temple and seeks him out. By including this in the story, John's Gospel gave the early church community the courage to face excommunication, promising them that in their isolation Jesus would seek them out. In reference to this verse, Brown makes an analogy between Jesus and the Hebrew depiction of Wisdom: "Wisdom is described as going about in search of those who are worthy of her and graciously appearing to them in their paths."[14] Jesus is like Wisdom, seeking out those who are worthy.

It is still unclear whether the man recognizes Jesus by sight as the one who cured him or whether he simply knows Jesus' name. Jesus' use of the term "Son of Man," as opposed to "Son of God" or "Messiah," is somewhat confusing here.

It would seem that the term "Son of Man" would not evoke the same images in the man's mind as these other more explicit terms denote.

*Verses 36-37:* The man confesses his ignorance of who the Son of Man is, and Jesus reveals his identity.

*Verse 38:* In this verse we reach the culmination of the man's growing awareness of who the person is who cured him. From the acknowledgment that it was the "man" Jesus, to the pronouncement that Jesus is a "prophet" and "from God," we now have his confession of "Lord, I believe" in response to Jesus' announcement that he is the Son of Man. Not only does the man come to believe, but he also worships Jesus. This final confession of faith may not have happened if Jesus had not sought him out.

In the final analysis, however, the man born blind is kicked out of the religious community, can no longer beg for a living, has no training, no work, and no new community (that we know about) that he can join. Unlike the Bartimaeus text, this text gives us no clue that the man born blind goes with Jesus and joins the group of disciples and followers. He is basically isolated and alone, but able to gaze with awe at the visual world around him.

## Scene 7 (Verses 39-41)

*Verse 39:* The Pharisees return as part of the background, overhearing this statement that Jesus makes: "I came into this world for judgment so that those who do not see may see, and those who do see may become blind." The first part of the sentence makes sense: "I came into this world . . . so that those who do not see may see." The second part, however, is much more cryptic: "[so that] those who do see may become blind." Is it that those who can see will *recognize* their inability or refusal to understand the divine nature of Jesus, or is it that Jesus intentionally (in some way) makes them *not* understand? And if the latter is true, why would

74

Jesus want people not to believe? One thing is clear, Jesus is using the term "blind" metaphorically. It is this section of the text that encourages the metaphorical or figurative use of "blindness" in relationship to those who are not believers, those who are "living in sin."

*Verse 40:* The Pharisees who have overheard Jesus' statement in verse 39 say "Surely we are not blind, are we?" Clearly they have the physical ability to see.

*Verse 41:* But Jesus responds "If you were blind, you would not have sin. But now that you say, 'We see,' your sin remains." Again, Jesus claims that those who think they see everything perfectly are really not understanding at all. And their lack of understanding and belief about Jesus' identity is equated with sin. The unique aspect about this verse, however, is that Jesus says that persons who are physically blind have *no* sin. This statement is surprising, especially when it is juxtaposed with the healing narratives that equate blindness or other disabilities *with* sin, and that equate being cured of one's blindness with having faith. On the one hand, it is an acknowledgment of the innocence of those who suffer through no fault of their own. On the other hand, in the same way that it is not true that all disability is the result of sin, it is likewise not true that persons who are blind are truly innocent and free from sin.

## Traditional Homiletic

I have heard this text preached in many different ways. There are so many elements involved that out of necessity preachers tend to focus on only one or two. Sermons often emphasize the theme of one's progression of faith, tracing the growth of the man's confession as he realizes just who Jesus is. Another focus is that of Jesus' triumph of light over darkness: Jesus as the light of and for the world. A common interpretation is the metaphorical one, in which the neighbors are "blind," the Pharisees are "blind," the parents are "blind," but the one born blind sees. Or, "only the man who realizes his own blindness can learn to see. Only the man who realizes his own sin can be forgiven."[15] Or, "life is blindness without Christ."[16] In all of these instances blindness is again equated with sin or with a broken relationship with God.

Some commentators encourage preachers to focus on the relation between physical suffering and sin, or on how suffering is sent to offer us a higher calling: "If tragedy or suffering comes to us, . . . we shall have to bear the pain; but what inexpressible folly not to accept the high vocation it was sent to offer us."[17] Others talk about the man's cure as his being "liberated from dependence," which clearly implies that dependence is something that is enslaving and to be avoided at all costs. But that assumes that people who can see are not dependent on anyone or anything, which is not true. And for those whom society labels as more dependent than others, we should focus on interdependency rather than on liberation from dependence.

An early church interpretation of this text related it to baptism. Artwork of the man born blind has been found in the catacombs, often in the context of a depiction of Christian baptism. This entire ninth chapter of the book of John was used as a reading in preparing candidates for baptism.[18] As the concept of original sin emerged, the text was interpreted to mean that the man was born in sin and that the sin had to be washed away in the waters of the pool or the waters of baptism. Blindness was associated with original sin, as Tertullian, in the opening of his tract on baptism, used blindness metaphorically: "The present work will treat of our sacrament of water which washes away the sins of our original blindness and sets us free unto eternal life."[19]

The theological interpretations of Jesus being the light of the world and the man's increasing confession, from Jesus as a man to Jesus as the Son of Man, can be preached without using blindness as a metaphor or symbol of sin. The preacher should also take care in using the images of light and darkness, so that these are not equated with blackness and whiteness in similar ways.

The metaphorical interpretation of blindness for sin, however, continues to oppress those who are blind. The early church's emphasis on baptism likewise connects blindness with sin. Although the baptism theme is one that was utilized by the early church, it is not part of the original text. So what other options are possible?

## A Healing Homiletic

Certainly Jesus seeking us out in our times of loneliness and rejection could be explored further. But there are a few interesting twists in this text that come out of a disability hermeneutic. The first is the answer of Jesus to the disciples' question that neither the man nor his parents sinned. This text's assertion that disability is not caused by sin goes against the implied theology of some of the other healing narratives.

A second interesting twist in this text is that the man's cure added to his isolation rather than giving him a sense of belonging. He was also untrained and unemployed. Major life changes often result in loss of community and identity, and the transition between losing one community and developing another may be a long one.

Another issue that arises is the contradiction to the theology that faith is needed before cure can take place. Here it is clear that the man did not have faith at the time of the cure. His faith developed as he began to articulate his experience to those who challenged him. Can we be about bringing healing to those who do not exemplify any faith? How would the church be different if we did not require confessions before we became actively involved in healing our world?

The Text
**Mark 10:46-52**

46They came to Jericho. As he and his disciples and a large crowd were leaving Jericho, Bartimaeus son of Timaeus, a blind beggar, was sitting by the roadside. 47When he heard that it was Jesus of Nazareth, he began to shout out and say, "Jesus, Son of David, have mercy on me!" 48Many sternly ordered him to be quiet, but he cried out even more loudly, "Son of David, have mercy on me!" 49Jesus stood still and said, "Call him here." And they called the blind man, saying to him, "Take heart; get up, he is calling you." 50So throwing off his cloak, he sprang up and came to Jesus. 51Then Jesus said to him, "What do you want me to do for you?" The blind man said to him, "My teacher, let me see again." 52Jesus said to him, "Go; your faith has made you well." Immediately he regained his sight and followed him on the way.

## *Hermeneutics*

This text is strategically placed by Mark. It provides a bookend to Jesus' wandering ministry, which began with the healing of another man who was blind in Mark 8:22-26. As the end of this central section of Mark's Gospel, it is also the bridge to Jesus' Jerusalem ministry. The story of Bartimaeus is the final healing narrative in the Gospel as a whole.

The story functions more as a legend than as a miracle story, because the focus is not so much on the miracle worker but rather on the legendary character Bartimaeus and his actions, which will "teach the reader what to emulate."[20] According to the text, the cure itself is uneventful. Jesus does not use spittle or any other physical element. He does not touch Bartimaeus; he only speaks and Bartimaeus can see.

This text also has the characteristics of a demand story: a subject (Bartimaeus) who demands something of the miracle worker, and an opposition that needs to be overcome (the crowd that tells Bartimaeus to be quiet).[21] Demand stories are also identified by a strong central character who takes an active role in overcoming the opposition.[22] In this text, Bartimaeus ignores the crowd's opposition and cries out even louder.

There are unique elements to this narrative that are not found elsewhere. It is the only healing text in which the person with the disability is named. His name, which denotes his relationship to his father—"son of Timaeus"—has been preserved by the community. Another unique element is that at the end of the narrative Bartimaeus becomes a follower of Jesus. This may be a story that explains how Bartimaeus became a disciple and well-known follower of Jesus.[23]

The Bartimaeus text takes place in Jericho, as Jesus and his disciples are passing through on their way to Jerusalem. The next chapter in Mark tells us that they are on their way to Jerusalem to celebrate Passover.[24]

Jesus and his followers, along with others going to Jerusalem, would have created a large group of people traveling together. The journey would become a parade of sorts. Those who could not make the journey would gather along the roadside to bid the travelers well. It is here that the story takes place—on the roadside. Along with those who are regularly there begging for alms to survive, a large crowd of villagers has gathered to watch the travelers pass by.

*Verse 46:* From the beginning of the narrative, we are told the man's name and his situation. Bartimaeus is blind, begs to survive, and spends his days by the roadside depending on others' compassion. He is on the edge of society, marginalized because of his condition.

*Verse 47:* Being blind, Bartimaeus would hear the commotion of many people passing by but would have no idea who they were. He hears the murmurings spreading through the crowd that among the travelers is Jesus of Nazareth. Not knowing exactly where in relation to himself Jesus is, he does not waste a second but begins immediately to call out Jesus' name: "Jesus, Son of David, have mercy on me!" He does not sit back pitying himself, waiting for someone to approach him and offer help. He takes responsibility for his own life and takes the initiative in assertively seeking what he feels he needs.

Why he uses the term "Son of David" is a puzzle. This title is introduced in this text in contrast to "Son of Man," the messianic term commonly used by Mark in the rest of the Gospel.[25] "Son of David" is used often by Matthew in his Gospel, but this is the only instance in the Gospel of Mark that the phrase is used as a title for Jesus. It is more probable that Bartimaeus referred to Jesus as Rabbi, and that "Son of David" is a later insertion.[26]

*Verse 48:* In this one verse we have a response from the crowd to Bartimaeus's cry and a counter-reply from Bartimaeus that is stronger than the first. The crowd views Bartimaeus's calling out to Jesus as rude at best. He is interrupting the procession and making a nuisance of himself. He is nothing. He should not act as if he is someone who deserves recognition, let alone attention. He should melt into the crowd and make himself invisible like a good blind beggar. When he cries out, the crowd orders him to be quiet as if he were a child who is misbehaving.

This is still true today. Persons who are blind and those with other disabilities are supposed to be invisible—out of sight, out of mind. Often treated as if they are children, they are expected to be quiet and passive rather than assertive or aggressive.

But Bartimaeus does not accept this role for himself. He does not play the passive role of someone to be pitied and taken care of, an invisible object by the roadside. No. He takes control of his life once again. He ignores those who think they are more important than he is, he rejects those who are telling him to shut up, and cries out even louder: "Jesus, Son of David, have mercy on me!"

Some scholars identify this movement in calling out as a "model of active faith,"[27] while others see it as a "venture of desperation, more a wild hope than of any considered faith."[28] Later, in verse 51, we learn that Bartimaeus at one time in his life could see. His blindness was a tremendous loss for him—different than it would be for someone blind from birth who knows only that existence. Bartimaeus knows what is possible both physically (seeing again) and, most important, socially (being a full, accepted member of the community again). His calling out is at the least an expression of hope that the rumors of Jesus' ability to cure people are true.

*Verse 49:* Instead of ignoring Bartimaeus's cry, Jesus stops in the middle of his journey and tells the people to inform Bartimaeus that he wants to talk to him. Jesus has a goal— arriving in Jerusalem. He is in the midst of a large group of people who are following him and pushing him toward that goal, but Jesus takes time out to recognize the presence of the one called Bartimaeus. The crowd wants to make Bartimaeus invisible, but Jesus makes him visible, and in doing so, acknowledges his humanity and offers him respect.

When Bartimaeus is recognized and made visible by someone important, suddenly the crowd changes its tone and likewise treats Bartimaeus respectfully. "Take heart; get up, he is calling you." Sometimes it just takes one person in leadership to provide the model of honoring those considered expendable by society to change the mood of the crowd.

*Verse 50:* Bartimaeus throws off his cloak as he jumps up and goes to Jesus. The cloak is important because Bartimaeus uses it in earning a living as a beggar: it functions as a first-century collection plate. Beggars would spread their cloaks out on the ground and people would place their alms in the cloak.[29] By throwing off his cloak, Bartimaeus is also risking the chance of not finding it again if he is still blind after his encounter with Jesus—if Jesus does not cure him.

How Bartimaeus finds Jesus is not clear from the text's description: "he sprang up and came to Jesus." Either the crowd has to lead him to Jesus or Jesus has to give him verbal cues for him to follow.

*Verse 51:* When Bartimaeus arrives where Jesus has stopped, Jesus does not assume anything. Bartimaeus does not become an object upon which Jesus displays his powers in front of all these people. Jesus treats the man as a person in his own right who has the ability to make his own decisions. Jesus asks him, "What do you want me to do for you?" In contrast to other healing narratives in which Jesus cures people without them knowing what is happening to them, this text describes Jesus taking the time to find out what the individual feels would be healing. Bartimaeus responds that he would like to "see again," which implies that he had become blind later in life. Bartimaeus becomes a participant in his own healing. He decides what would be healing for him.

Too often we make decisions for others who we feel are helpless or incapable of making their own decisions. We decide what is healing for them, when in reality what healing means for us may be oppressive to them. In this text, Jesus lets Bartimaeus decide for himself.

*Verse 52:* It is not until this last verse that Mark has Jesus speak the words that effect the cure and the proof that Bartimaeus has regained his sight. No physical elements are used in the process, simply the words from Jesus: "Go; your faith has made you well." Both "faith" and the Greek root of "made well" raise some questions and hermeneutical problems for persons with disabilities.

Because faith is identified as the cause or reason for Jesus' willingness to cure Bartimaeus, homileticians have preached the necessity for persons with disabilities to likewise have enough faith. And if they have enough faith, they too, like Bartimaeus, will be cured. And of course the reverse is also true. If they do not have enough faith, they will not be cured.

But what does faith really mean in this context? Commentators over the years have differed in their interpretation of what Jesus means when he says, "Your faith has made you well." Most contemporary scholars tend to believe that the statement does not refer to faith in the divinity of Jesus, since the origins of these narratives are preresurrection. One scholar says that Jesus was "identifying [Bartimaeus's] stubbornness as faith,"[30] while another says that in this text "faith does not mean credulity in Jesus' miracles but means something like power to meet the crisis in confidence."[31] Noting the similarity of Bartimaeus's persistence to that of the Syrophoenician woman, another scholar says that faith means not only confidence in Jesus' ability, but also Bartimaeus's "persistence in getting his attention."[32] Unlike the story of the man born blind, in John 9, in which the man's faith evolves after the cure, Mark's healing narratives imply at least some kind of faith prior to the cure.[33]

The healing narratives in the Gospel of Mark carry with them both the metaphorical interpretation of blindness and deafness and the connection between faith and cure. Today, the issue of faith in relation to healing is a complicated one. On the one hand, there is no doubt that the faith of persons with disabilities sustains many in their daily existence and is a healing element in their lives. On the other hand, to judge a person's faith (either what the person believes or the degree to which the person believes) and to make physical cure the criteria of that judgment is to erect barriers between persons with disabilities and God—to destroy faith.

In addition to the question of the meaning of "faith" in this verse is the issue of the Greek word that is translated "made well." *Sozein* can mean "heal," "make well," "save," "deliver," or "protect." *Sozein* is used in reference to the alleviation of alienation from God and others caused by all these factors. Because it is used to mean both healing and forgiveness of sins, the correlation has often been made between blindness and sin or lack of faith, and between seeing and faith or salvation. Salvation is often equated with seeing, moving from darkness into light, and in this text, the restoration of sight by Jesus.[34] As I have already noted, the metaphorical usage of blindness as a symbol of sin and lack of faith is oppressive. According to this interpretation, a person who continues to be blind cannot receive salvation, for salvation is only for those who see. The fine line between metaphor and reality is blurred in our interpretation of this text.

Finally, we are informed in this verse that Bartimaeus "followed him on the way." Unlike other persons who are healed by Jesus, Bartimaeus becomes an active disciple of Jesus. From being found "by the roadside" to being "on the way," Bartimaeus moves from being marginalized to being an active participant.

## Traditional Homiletic

Like the John 9 text, the Bartimaeus text has commonly been subject to a problematic metaphorical interpretation. There is a similar comparison between light and darkness— "we must allow Jesus to bring us out of darkness and into the light"[35]—implying that blindness and darkness are out of the range of God. As they have done with John 9, commentators of the Bartimaeus text have identified prebelieving states of existence and a refusal to recognize the christological identity of Jesus with blindness:

> . . . the gospel of Christ crucified and the challenge to live a life following the way of the cross is the cure for that blindness.[36]

> . . . only a "blind" man would call Jesus Son of David. He is really Son of God.[37]

Homiletical emphasis is also given to Mark's perspective that the disciples lack an understanding of who Jesus is. The congregation is compared to the disciples and blindness is used metaphorically to describe this situation:

> . . . all disciples share the blindness of the disciples except when Jesus opens their eyes to understand.[38]

. . . blindness must be healed if one is to understand and follow Jesus on his way.[39]

. . . only if the disciples/reader struggles against the internal demons that render us deaf and mute, . . . only if we can recognize our blindness and seek true vision—then can the discipleship adventure carry on.[40]

Another metaphorical interpretation of this text is sometimes suggested for preaching. This one proposes that we all have some "bad habit" or some "wrong things" in our lives that we need to abandon as Bartimaeus did.[41] Blindness is a symbol of one of these "bad habits." This likewise equates blindness with the "wrong things" in our lives (in other words, sin).

## A Healing Homiletic

This text also offers us two positive examples. The first is Bartimaeus himself, who is raised up as an example of true discipleship. Unfortunately, this too can be used metaphorically. As one scholar states, "Bartimaeus serves as a prototype of the true disciple and provides a model for the Christian who needs to know what it means to see and be saved."[42] Seeing is still identified as a prerequisite for salvation and true discipleship. The second example we have is that of Jesus, who takes the time to recognize and pay attention to one deemed outcast by society. He provides a model not only for serving others but also for treating "even the least of these" with respect.

What other possibilities are there as preachers attempt to be faithful to the text and not oppressive for persons who are blind today? Preachers can use the text to address the situation of those who are marginalized today—whom society and the church try to keep invisible. They are treated as children and ordered to keep silent. If the status quo is to be maintained, their passivity is essential. When they cry out or take control of their lives and do not wait to be approached or helped, society is not pleased with their behavior. Chaos often ensues. We saw this on a large scale with the Los Angeles uprising and recognize this phenomenon in smaller degrees all around us.

There is also the power issue involved when those who feel they are more important than others, better than others, try to control those on the margins. But when a respected leader in the community models something different, the crowd changes its attitude and its behavior as well.

For those with disabilities, the Bartimaeus text is a great example of speaking up in whatever form, taking control of one's life, and being an active participant in one's own healing process and in the service of ministry.

# CHAPTER FOUR

# Deafness and Hearing Loss

As often as other disabilities are mentioned in the New Testament, it seems odd that Mark 7:31-37 is the only text that narrates the story of a person with deafness.[1] The other two texts that mention deafness in general show Jesus to be the fulfillment of the promise of Isaiah 35:5-6: "Go and tell John what you hear and see: the blind receive their sight, the lame walk, the lepers are cleansed, the deaf hear, the dead are raised, and the poor have good news brought to them" (Matt. 11:4-5; see also Luke 7:22). Isaiah 29:18 also proclaims that "On that day the deaf shall hear the words of a scroll," and Leviticus 19:14 warns people: "You shall not revile the deaf or put a stumbling block before the blind." But the New Testament is relatively silent about persons who are deaf. This one text, then, carries a lot of weight for those who are deaf seeking biblical guidance.

The lectionary pericope also includes verses 24-30, which tell the story of the Syrophoenician woman and her daughter. Because this narrative is more about the exchange between the mother and Jesus than about the healing or exorcism, I will not deal with it here.

## Deafness and Hearing Loss

Several years ago, I was pastor of a deaf church in Maryland. Most of the deaf people[2] in the congregation were born deaf and communicated in some form of sign language. The deaf church rented space from a hearing congregation, since we did not have our own building. One member of the hearing church was very concerned about the deaf people who shared their facilities. Whenever a faith healer came to the nearest city, this woman wanted to take all the deaf people to the healing services so that they could be "healed." To be healed, in her mind, meant to be cured of their deafness. She was shocked when the deaf people had no interest in going, not only because they did not trust faith healers, but because they did not want to be "hearing." Those within the Deaf Culture (mostly those who were born deaf and raised by deaf parents) see themselves more as a cultural, linguistic minority group, similar to Korean Americans or Mexican Americans, than as persons with disabilities. They have their own language, values, and customs that are integral to their culture. They often reject the term "disability" in reference to their deafness because the term implies that there is something wrong that needs "fixing."[3]

On the other hand, many persons who become hard of hearing later in life are very interested in a cure for their hearing loss. They have lost something that has been very precious to them—the sounds of children laughing, of birds chirping, of an orchestra playing a Mozart symphony, the ease of daily conversation. They grew up taking for granted the ability to hear spoken language and the ability to be understood when they spoke. They miss what they used to have and go to great lengths to get back as much hearing as possible through hearing aids, cochlear implants, and other assistive listening devices. For them, "healing" may or may not mean "cure." What *is* healing is being able to maintain one's relationships with family and community, and for that to happen, adjustments have to be made by all.

Today, there is no easy way to talk about persons who have a hearing loss. Each person's experience is unique, requiring various descriptions. There is no one term that encompasses all those with hearing loss. Not only are there audiological differences that range between mild hearing loss and profound deafness, but there are also linguistic and cultural differences that contribute to the tremendous complexity one faces when dealing with hearing loss.

The linguistic differences revolve around whether a person's primary language is American Sign Language, a sign language based on the English language, or "oralism"—speechreading and speaking English.[4] There is also a manual code of phonetic sounds in the English language called Cued Speech.

The cultural differences are determined by which language is used. If American Sign Language is the primary language (preferably a native language), the person is considered "Culturally Deaf." If English is the primary language, then the person is considered "Culturally Hearing."

Linguistic and therefore cultural orientation is usually determined early in a deaf child's life, through choice of educational placement—in a deaf residential school, a bilingual/bicultural program, a mainstreamed, total communication program, or an oral program. Those who grew up hearing, with English as their first language, will always be culturally hearing. A good indication of cultural orientation is whether one uses a spoken language or American Sign Language as his or her primary mode of communication.

The complexity of this group of persons with hearing loss is further complicated by the fact that one's cultural and linguistic identity does not always correlate with the degree of one's audiological deafness. Marjorie, on the one hand, lost her hearing late in life and is audiologically profoundly deaf, but she identifies herself as hard of hearing because she is culturally hearing, does not sign, and continues to use English as her primary language. David, on the other hand, is audiologically mildly hard of hearing, but was born to deaf parents. His first language was American Sign Language, and he is culturally deaf.

In addition to hearing loss, deafness has historically (and biblically) been associated with one's ability to speak well. In the past (and unfortunately, sometimes still today), deaf people who chose not to use their voices were referred to as "deaf and dumb." In reality, however, there are very few deaf people who are also mute. Mute means unable to make sounds or to speak. Deaf people have the physical ability to speak, but because they cannot hear how to pronounce words, they often sound unintelligible. Many choose not to use their voices to speak because people over the years have equated unintelligible sounds with lack of intelligence (hence the evolution of the word *dumb* from meaning "lacking in intelligence," to also meaning "unable to speak"). Although much has happened to improve the quality of life for persons who are deaf, deafened, and hard of hearing, many still struggle in society today. Technology has made many advances in recent years: devices that communicate over the phone through the printed text instead of voice; doorbells that flash a light instead of ring a bell; machines that provide captions for certain television programs; hearing aids; and even cochlear implants. But all of these are expensive. Deaf people depend on machines and interpreters to facilitate communication with the hearing world.

Even with all the technology, misunderstandings are still common. Sally felt ignored because she asked her fiancé a question, but he didn't answer her. Being hard of hearing, he simply had not heard her question. Deafened in adulthood, Jane has a hard time monitoring her own speech now. One day while she was shopping she asked a salesclerk the price of a dress several times, but the salesclerk did not have the patience or take the time to try to understand her. A policeman shouted "Stop!" to Jim, but Jim, being totally deaf, kept on walking. The policeman, continuing to yell, approached Jim from behind and slapped handcuffs on him. With his hands restrained, Jim had no way to communicate.

Miscommunication is even more common with deaf persons who immigrate here from other countries. They have difficulty finding people who know their native country's sign language in order to facilitate not only basic communication, but also the learning of American Sign Language and written English.

The age at which hearing loss occurs, the tremendous range of audiological differences, from mild hearing loss to profound deafness, the variety of linguistic preferences, the array of cultural orientations, and the decision to use one's voice or not all make deafness and hearing loss a very complex issue. These complexities are not only part of today's deaf, deafened, and hard of hearing communities; they are also a part of the narrative in Mark 7, in which Jesus heals a deaf man.

The Text
**Mark 7:31-37**

> [31]Then he returned from the region of Tyre, and went by way of Sidon towards the Sea of Galilee, in the region of the Decapolis. [32]They brought to him a deaf

man who had an impediment in his speech; and they begged him to lay his hand on him. [33]He took him aside in private, away from the crowd, and put his fingers into his ears, and he spat and touched his tongue. [34]Then looking up to heaven, he sighed and said to him, "Ephphatha," that is, "Be opened." [35]And immediately his ears were opened, his tongue was released, and he spoke plainly. [36]Then Jesus ordered them to tell no one; but the more he ordered them, the more zealously they proclaimed it. [37]They were astounded beyond measure, saying, "He has done everything well; he even makes the deaf to hear and the mute to speak."

## Hermeneutics

This text is unique to Mark. None of the other Gospels include this narrative. It is also unique in that this is the only place in the Bible that the Aramaic word *ephphatha* is found. A foreign phrase for the formulaic command "Be Opened," *ephphatha* conjures up magical phrases similar to our "Open Sesame" or "Abracadabra,"[5] and conveys a notion of mysterious power. Jesus also uses a physical element in the healing—spittle. The use of the physical element in healing is characteristic of the "pure form of a Hellenistic wonder story."[6] The fact that the story of the healing of the deaf man is found only in Mark may be due to the use in the text of matter as well as the spoken word to effect the healing. Subsequent Synoptic Gospel writers "preferred to depict him as healing solely through a word."[7]

Within the deaf community, controversy has arisen over verse 32, which says "They brought to him a deaf man who had an *impediment in his speech*." It is clear here that, contrary to traditional interpretation, this man was not mute. He had use of his vocal chords.

While the term "deaf" implies audiological deafness, the phrase "impediment in his speech" implies that the man could speak and be understood, but did not have "normal" speech. This suggests that he was either hard of hearing or deafened after having learned speech, rather than born totally deaf. If he was totally deaf from birth, probably his speech would have been *unintelligible*, not simply impeded. Commentators who suggest that the man stuttered[8] misunderstand the connection between lack of hearing and inability to enunciate. Stuttering in combination with deafness is an extremely rare occurrence.

Although verse 32 seems to imply that the man was deafened later in life or hard of hearing, historically this text was used against the signing deaf community. This "Ephphatha" text was used by well-meaning hearing clergy and educators as proof that it was God's will that deaf people speak and speechread rather than sign. It was the rationale needed to forbid deaf people to use sign language and force them (often by physical abuse) to speak verbally. This text became one of the foundations of the "oralism" movement that taught deaf children to communicate solely by lipreading/speechreading ("hearing through the eyes") and speaking. Since a person's deafness could not be healed, despite abusive attempts, misinterpreters of this text took it as a mandate to teach deaf people how to speak. "We are all children of the one Christ who gave us the example. . . . The minister of Christ must open the mouth of the deaf."[9]

Deaf communities and schools, as well as the National Association of the Deaf, were in existence long before the edict of the Conference of Milan, Italy, in 1880, which forbade sign language in favor of oralism. Deaf people took great offense at such comments from international hearing clergy and educators who were not familiar with their culture or language.[10]

Consequently, this text has very negative and oppressive implications for some. On the other hand, many within the signing deaf community have tried to reclaim this text as a symbol of assurance that Jesus cares about them. The term *ephphatha* ("be opened"), found in verse 34, is used in several deaf religious contexts. *Be Opened* is the title of one of the first books on deaf ministry,[11] and "Mark 7" is the name of a well-known religious deaf camp. A careful analysis of this text's redemptive and oppressive possibilities is crucial in deciding how to preach on the cure of the deaf man.

*Verse 31:* The exact geographical journey is highly improbable, since Sidon was north of Tyre and Galilee was southeast. The order of Mark's Gospel is based on the subjects of the various pericopes rather than precise geography. Often these journeying verses are merely transitional sentences from one event in the life of Jesus to another.

*Verse 32:* Traditionally this narrative has been called "The Healing of the Deaf-Mute," but as was noted earlier, the man was clearly not mute. It is important to note that Mark says "they" brought the deaf man to Jesus. We do not know who "they" were, and we have no indication that the deaf man knew what was going on.

*Verse 33:* This verse is somewhat controversial. If the man was hard of hearing, taking him aside in private might have moved him away from all the background noise and assisted him in understanding what Jesus was trying to say. For those in the deaf community who use sign language, however, this act is also reminiscent of needing to "sign" in private, to hide one's signs so that one is not labeled as animalistic and barbaric by others. According to commentator William Barclay, Jesus took the deaf man aside because "Deaf folk are always a little embarrassed. In some ways it is more embarrassing to be deaf than it is to be blind. A deaf person knows he cannot hear; and when someone in a crowd shouts at him and tries to make him hear, in his excitement he becomes all the more helpless."[12] In reality, however, the ones who look foolish are those who shout at a person who cannot hear.

The text says that Jesus puts his fingers into the deaf man's ears. Some commentators see this as Jesus using gestures or signs and therefore as Jesus trying to communicate with the deaf man on his own terms: "[G]estures are the only way in which Jesus can speak to the deaf-mute," writes Eduard Schweizer;[13] William Barclay writes, "[T]hroughout the whole miracle Jesus acted what he was going to do in dumb-show. He put his hands in the man's ears and touched his tongue with spittle."[14] But sticking one's fingers into another's ears and touching another's tongue with spittle are not gestures. They are *actions* done by one to another. Some may even consider them invasive actions—particularly if the man who was deaf had not granted permission. The act of laying hands on another's head or shoulders can be seen as a blessing and much less threatening. That is what the people who accompanied the man who was deaf begged Jesus to do, although Mark tells us he does otherwise.

The use of spittle has a unique connection with the narrative of the man from Bethsaida who was blind (Mark 8:22-26). These are the only two texts that say Jesus uses spittle to effect a cure. It is important to note that saliva was considered to be pollutive.[15] It was a bodily excretion that could cause a person to be ritually unclean (see chapter 6). But Jesus challenges the purity codes. Instead of Jesus becoming unclean, the "contagion is reversed and the gentile healed."[16] This method of using spittle was adopted by the baptismal rite of early Christianity. "The bishop or presiding officer conducting the baptism would spit on his fingers, then touch them to the candidate's ears, eyes, and mouth, symbolizing the person's new ability to hear the Gospel and witness to his or her faith."[17]

*Verse 34:* Looking up to heaven is a gesture that anyone might understand on some level. Even today in American Sign Language, signs for God and heaven are spatially "up"— above the body. The text also says that Jesus sighed before he said "Ephphatha." One author relates this sigh to a struggle with evil forces: "The word translated 'sighed' is used by Paul in Romans 8:22-26 and 2 Corinthians 5:2-4 to express an intense struggle of the soul. Apparently Jesus was contending with the whole host of demonic powers in effecting this cure."[18] But equating Jesus' sigh with a struggle with demonic powers implies that it was demon possession that caused the person's deafness. Biddle agrees with this assessment when he says that it was "the power of Satan which caused the impairments."[19]

Nowhere in this text or any other Gospel text, however, is there any connection between deafness and demon possession. There are texts that describe a person with a demon who is also mute (Matt. 9:32-33, 12:22; Luke 11:14; Mark 9:17) but none where the person is also deaf.[20] Unfortunately, many people today still hold this opinion regarding persons who are deaf—that there must be something evil about them or they would not be deaf. Although Jesus took the man aside, his use of the term *ephphatha* is clearly for the crowd or Mark's audience. It is not for the deaf man, who cannot hear it. And saying it in an unfamiliar language makes it all the more impossible for the deaf man to speechread what Jesus is saying. One scholar says that "no doubt Jesus would have to shout it [ephphatha] out loudly, so that the deaf man might hear it";[21] but speechreading does not work this way. Rather than making words clearer, shouting usually distorts sounds beyond visual recognition.

*Verse 35:* According to the text, the cure happens immediately. The man's ears are opened and he can hear; his tongue is released and he can speak clearly. The order is appropriate, since speaking clearly is dependent on one's ability to hear how to pronounce sounds.

This verse, along with those that relate the healing of the persons who were blind and the man who was paralyzed, completes the fulfillment of Isaiah's vision of the coming day of salvation found in Isaiah 35:5-6a: "Then the eyes of the blind shall be opened, and the ears of the deaf unstopped; then the lame shall leap like a deer, and the tongue of the speechless sing for joy."

*Verse 36:* It is typical in Mark's Gospel for Jesus to tell the people not to speak about what they have seen, and for the people to speak about it anyway. Yet it is particularly curious in this text, for the man has received the ability to speak clearly, but Jesus bids him to be silent. Instead of being able to speak about what has happened to him, he is ordered by Jesus to be silent and tell no one.

*Verse 37:* This closing statement is about the power of Jesus and what that might reveal about who he is. It is Jesus' actions ("he has done everything well; he even makes the deaf to hear and the mute to speak") that point to his identity. Mark is leading his audience to Peter's confession in chapter 8: "You are the Messiah." However, as Eduard Riegert and Richard H. Hiers have pointed out, "there are no Jewish traditions to the effect that the Messiah would heal."[22]

## *Traditional Homiletic*

As in many of the healing narratives, faith becomes a central element in preaching these texts. About the story of the healing of the deaf man we find conflicting opinions from the commentators. One says that "the man found wholeness of body and spirit because of his faith in Jesus,"[23] while another says that "the man's deafness prevented him from hearing the voice of Jesus, which in others was able to awaken expectant faith."[24] Theologically, the one implies that the deaf man needed to have faith—and enough of it—in order to be healed. The other says that he could not have faith because he could not hear, and faith comes by hearing. In reality, however, the word or concept of faith never appears in this text. According to the narrative, there is no indication that the man knows anything about Jesus at all.

This notion that hearing is required for faith comes in part from Romans 10:17—"Faith comes by hearing"—and was emphasized by Luther in the Protestant Reformation:

> God no longer requires the feet or the hands or any other member; He requires only the ears. . . . For if you ask a Christian what the work is by which he becomes worthy of the name "Christian," he will be able to give absolutely no other answer than that it is the hearing of the Word of God, that is, faith. Therefore the ears alone are the organs of a Christian man, for he is justified and declared to be a Christian, not because of the works of any members but because of faith.[25]

It is this notion that hearing is required for faith that makes this text potentially destructive for those in the deaf community. If Jesus had to cure the person's deafness in order for that person to "have faith" and "be saved," then is faith denied to all those who are deaf today? The man's newfound

99

ability to speak in the text has also been interpreted over the years as a sign that speech was also necessary, not so much for faith, but in order to be made in the image of God: "I will state some preliminary axioms of indisputable truth, by which it will be shown from the nature of God that creatures formed in God's image ought of necessity be able to speak and in this respect resemble their Creator."[26]

Today it should seem obvious that hearing is not necessary for faith and that speech is not what makes us in the image of God. And yet these concepts are still encouraged by prominent homileticians: Craddock states repeatedly that "the event of the Word of God needs the ear, for faith comes by hearing."[27] Buttrick concurs when he says "If 'faith comes from hearing,' then we must strive to be heard."[28] Brueggemann states that "it is speech and only speech that bonds God and human creatures."[29] As commentators provide guidance for preachers concerning the interpretation of this text for contemporary congregations, preachers, too, pick up on these same images. Biddle says "it is only as the church hears the word of God that it has a message to speak."[30] By focusing on hearing as essential for faith and speech as necessary to be in the image of God, the church makes a clear proclamation to millions of deaf and mute people around the world—"you are not a child of God; you do not belong here." That is not healing.[31]

Other homileticians choose to preach this text metaphorically. The language used assumes that all deaf persons are poor, living in bonds of oppression because of their disability, and in need of salvation, which implies that their condition is due to some evil or sin from which they need to be saved. Riegert and Hiers write that "To be 'taken aside from the multitude, privately,'" is to "experience the full bewilderment of our deafness and muteness and the horrifying reality of our isolation. It is there, when we 'hit bottom,' that we may finally hear, and finally find fumbling words: 'I was on the road to dissolution, but now I may begin again. Praise God!' There faith is created again."[32] Although it is probably true that persons with disabilities in the first century had no way to earn a living, were poor, and saw their lives as oppressed, to equate deafness and muteness with "horrifying isolation" and "hitting bottom" is exceptionally dehumanizing for those who live with deafness and muteness as daily realities. This is the danger of using deafness and muteness metaphorically.

Consider the implications of these other quotations from the commentaries that use deafness as a metaphor: "The ills of the earth are due largely to the spiritual deafness of those who cannot hear the 'still, sad music of humanity' or the 'still small voice' of God."[33] People "are too deaf to catch the sobs of grief . . . too hard of hearing, to catch the rumble of discontent over injustice."[34] According to these uses of deafness as a metaphor, the evils of the world, poverty, and most injustices are due to our "deafness."

What is really intended by these phrases is an indictment against those within our congregations and within our society who refuse to pay attention to or who intentionally ignore the call of God or the cries of those in need, or those who refuse to work against injustice. That message can be preached without using "deafness" and "muteness" to describe this condition. Whether we *choose* to preach this message as a result of our reading of this particular text is another matter. The man who is deaf in this text does not exhibit any of these "sinful" behaviors. In the story itself, he is not there as a "bad example" of how we should not be. We have no background into his understanding of God, his knowledge of Jesus, or his religious faith. He is simply a deaf man who is brought to Jesus for "healing" or "cure."

To make the connection between the message of ignoring the call of God and the cries of those in need and the story of the deaf man, we must jump from the story of a man who is physically *incapable* of hearing to an analogy that says we (like him?) *refuse* to listen. I realize that for many the distinction seems almost unnoticeable and this is a very small hop. But for some, it is a gigantic leap. We are not "like him." We can hear but we *choose* to ignore.

This metaphorical interpretation is encouraged by the commentaries because of the common understanding that the story itself functions as a metaphor and was part of Mark's literary intent in including this story in the Gospel. Mark intended the story to show how stubborn and dense the disciples are in understanding who Jesus is. And the cure of the deaf man was Mark's attempt at trying to "convert" the disciples to a new way of being in the world. The preacher who chooses this interpretation for his or her sermon should avoid using the terms "deafness" and "muteness" (and certainly "dumbness") in the language of the sermon. In other words, the preacher should refrain from using the words that identify the physical reality of some to describe the sinful behavior of others.

## A Healing Homiletic

Consider using a different metaphorical interpretation that would deal with the community's isolation of the person with the disability just because of who he is, rather than linking the man's disability with any "sinful behaviors," which are not in the text. This approach to the text would treat the person as a subject in his own right and would also recognize the various ways cultures ostracize people who do not fit the norm.

Our own culture rejects those who are of a different skin color than what the ruling class perceives to be the norm. We ostracize those who are not physically "up to par" with societal standards that are often set by the media. We punish those whose sexual orientations are different from what some consider to be "normal." We isolate and ostracize people because of who they are, not always by what they do. People in the congregation may be those who feel rejected by society, or the congregation may be part of the privileged class who decides the boundaries and does the ostracizing. What does the healing touch of Jesus mean in your particular context?

In this text we also find Jesus healing before any demonstration of faith on the part of the deaf man. Can we be so bold as to offer healing freely to isolated individuals and our wounded world without requiring faith as a prerequisite?

CHAPTER FIVE

# Paralysis

There are only two stories in the Gospels that deal with specific persons who are paralyzed. Matthew 8:5-13 tells the story of the centurion's servant who is paralyzed, but Luke's version (Luke 7:1-10) makes no mention of the servant's paralysis, only that he "is ill and close to death" (v. 2). The story included in the lectionary is found in Mark 2:1-12 (with parallels in Matt. 9:1-8 and Luke 5:17-26). This is the familiar text of the man who is lowered through the roof of a house in order to be cured by Jesus.[1]

In addition to these stories, there are other general references in the Gospels to persons who are paralyzed in relationship to large groups of people who approach Jesus in hopes of being cured (Matt. 15:30-31, 21:14). John includes those who are paralyzed along with those who are blind and "lame" as among the people who wait at the Sheep Gate to enter the pool that is supposed to have curative powers (John 5:3). In the Gospel of Mark, however, the story of the man who was lowered through the roof is the only text that deals with a person who is paralyzed.

## Paralysis

Paralysis is an inability to move particular limbs or muscles of one's body. In flaccid forms of paralysis, the limbs are limp and flexible. In spastic forms of paralysis, the paralyzed parts of the body are stiff. Paraplegia and quadri-

104

plegia are the most well-known forms of paralysis. These types of paralysis are caused by disease of or injury to the spinal cord. Paraplegia is paralysis from the waist down, which usually means the person can move the head and arms but not the legs. Quadriplegia is commonly known as paralysis of the legs, arms, and trunk. However, spinal cord injuries vary depending on the cervical, thoracic, or lumbar level at which the damage takes place. While injury to cervical levels C4-8 results in what is considered quadriplegia, those with damage at the C5-6 levels often do have some movement capabilities. This movement is not voluntary, since the arms are paralyzed, but the arms can be supported so that changes in head position and the use of "body english" result in the hand being raised or lowered.[2] This minor movement is sometimes enough to operate the joystick of an electrical wheelchair. Mouthsticks are often used in typing, writing, dialing, and so forth.

Those with damage at the C4-5 levels require assistance for basic grooming activities but can often operate a computer and an electrical wheelchair with pneumatically ("sip-and-puff" method) controlled equipment or adaptive devices controlled by the mouth.[3] The movement possibilities vary from person to person depending on the extent and exact site of the injury to the spinal cord. Those with quadriplegia may or may not be able to speak.

Another common form of paralysis is hemiplegia, which is total or partial paralysis of the right side or left side of the body, caused by injury to the motor centers of the brain. Strokes can often cause forms of hemiplegia. Besides those who have paraplegia, quadriplegia, and hemiplegia, there are also persons who experience a complete but temporary paralysis, persons who have partial paralysis in one or more limbs, and persons who have paralysis of certain muscles of the body. Because the experience of those who have temporary or partial paralysis is drastically different from those who have paraplegia or quadriplegia, this chapter will be limited to the issues facing those who live daily with some kind of permanent, complete paralysis. It also needs to be noted that those who have quadriplegia deal with life very differently than do those with paraplegia, since being able to move one's arms and head and being able to speak makes independent living much more feasible. Those who have quadriplegia are often limited to the muscles available in their head and mouth to control their wheelchairs and communicate. For those with C4-5 damage, some form of attendant care is necessary for basic aspects of daily survival. Whether one can speak or not is another distinction that affects how society reacts to a person who is paralyzed.

Most persons who have paraplegia or quadriplegia are not born paralyzed. Eighty percent of spinal cord injuries occur in persons under the age of forty-five, with twenty-five as the median age.[4] Usually, accidents of some kind cause the injury to the spinal cord, which means that there is a period of physical rehabilitation (usually 84-116 days) in a hospital or rehabilitation center.[5] Basic psychological adjustment usually takes a couple of years. Dealing with the denial, depression, grief, and anger is a continual process.

Learning interdependency can be difficult. At the beginning of one's rehabilitative process, one's self-perception moves through transitions. Many young adults living active lives perceive themselves as being fiercely independent and even indestructible. In the prime of their lives, they seldom ponder their own mortality. As one enters the stage of rehabilitation, independence seems impossible. Dependency seems to be the norm, and lack of control over one's body often manifests itself in persons feeling they are of no use to others, which makes interdependency difficult to fathom. In the beginning it seems to people who are paralyzed that they are totally dependent on others, and they often question what they have to offer in return. While with proper support services independent living is possible for many, some degree of dependency will always be a reality. For some, it is dependency on people such as social workers and those who provide attendant care, on either a voluntary or paid basis. For all persons who experience paralysis of their limbs, there is dependency on various kinds of equipment: manual or electric wheelchairs, communication boards for those who cannot speak, lifts in vans or buses for transportation, and elevators, to name just a few. And for most, there is dependency on certain institutional systems that provide support services, such as Social Security, social services, vocational rehabilitation, and the medical profession at various levels.

One frustration is that the people, equipment and services one depends upon are not always depend*able*. Each one is important for daily survival—but beyond the control of the person who is paralyzed. Not being able to control those parts of one's body that are paralyzed is frustrating enough. But added to that is often the inability to control those parts of one's surroundings that make life not only survivable but meaningful. Both factors are constant reminders of the level of dependency, which others do not have to struggle with on a daily basis. The people and things one depends upon are often inconsistent, and one's own energy levels are also inconsistent. It is difficult to plan ahead when so often the only thing one can depend upon is inconsistency itself.

Dependency on ramps, lifts, and elevators for access into buildings should be more consistent since the passing of the Americans with Disabilities Act (ADA), but not all buildings are accessible; the ramps that do exist are often too steep or rough, and inside the building, restrooms and other facilities are not always accessible. Since religious institutions are exempt from the ADA, most churches are not welcoming communities for persons who are paralyzed. One look at the steps leading to the front door is a powerful enough message that a person who uses a wheelchair is not wanted as a part of the community. If a church does have a ramp for access into the sanctuary, often the fellowship hall or other rooms in the building are not accessible, and seldom is the chancel area or choir loft made accessible. While it may be possible for one to attend worship services, full participation in social activities and committee meetings, as well as the opportunity to be a liturgist, communion server, or choir member, is often out of the question. There is an implied assumption in both the church and society that persons who are paralyzed have little to offer. It is assumed that the giving is one-sided: services are provided *for* them but we do not often utilize the gifts persons who are paralyzed have to offer us.

Not being treated as an equal member of the community, either by the church or society, is one of the biggest barriers people who are paralyzed face. Being treated as a second-class citizen or even as being less than whole (i.e., human) is common. Being unable to move is often interpreted as being incapable in other areas as well. Persons who are paralyzed are often perceived as asexual beings, as their manhood and womanhood is questioned. Often treated as children, they must constantly struggle to be taken seriously as they attempt to participate in the decisions that affect their lives.

In the Mark 2 text of the man who was paralyzed, we do not know whether the man participated in the decision that changed his entire life or not.

The Text
**Mark 2:1-12**

[1]When he returned to Capernaum after some days, it was reported that he was at home. [2]So many gathered around that there was no longer room for them, not even in front of the door; and he was speaking the word to them. [3]Then some people came, bringing to him a paralyzed man, carried by four of them. [4]And when they could not bring him to Jesus because of the crowd, they removed the roof above him; and after having dug through it, they let down the mat on which the paralytic lay. [5]When Jesus saw their faith, he said to the paralytic, "Son, your sins are forgiven." [6]Now some of the scribes were sitting there, questioning in their hearts, [7]"Why does this fellow speak in this way? It is blasphemy! Who can forgive sins but God alone?" [8]At once Jesus perceived in his spirit that they were discussing these questions among themselves; and he said to them, "Why do you raise such questions in your hearts? [9]Which is easier, to say to the paralytic, 'Your sins are forgiven,' or to say, 'Stand up and take your mat and walk'? [10]But so that you may know that the Son of Man has authority on earth to forgive sins"—he said to the paralytic—[11]"I say to you,

> stand up, take your mat and go to your home."
> [12]And he stood up, and immediately took the mat and went out before all of them; so that they were all amazed and glorified God, saying, "We have never seen anything like this!"

## Hermeneutics

This text is found in the section of Mark that includes eight other controversy stories (Mark 2:1–3:35). All of these stories deal with Jesus and the conflicts that arise between him and the religious authorities. Whether the controversy is over healing on the sabbath or eating with tax collectors and sinners, the controversy narratives show how Jesus challenged traditional social and religious norms. In this text, the controversy with the scribes is over who has the authority to forgive sins. And it is this forgiveness of sins section that is problematic for persons with disabilities.

While in the John 9 text Jesus denies any causal relationship between the man's blindness and his sins, in this text Jesus says to the man who is paralyzed, "your sins are forgiven" (v. 5). The uniqueness of this text is that, as Gowan has noted, it "is the only healing story in which forgiveness of sin appears."[6] While Gowan believes that "Jesus does not speak of sin and sickness in a cause-and-effect way, for he only compares forgiveness and healing rather than equating them,"[7] a common assumption behind the interpretation of this text is that there is a physical cause-and-effect relationship between the forgiveness of the man's sins and the man's miraculous cure.

Because many scholars believe that the controversy over the forgiveness of sins (vv. 5b-10) is a later insertion to the older healing story,[8] it is tempting to dismiss the "forgiveness of sins" controversy with the scribes and deal only with the healing part of the narrative. But since this text is often used as justification for the theology that sin is the cause of disability, it is important to include it in the discussion here.

One of the common explanations for suffering in first-century Palestine was that it was a punishment for some form of transgression or sin. It was not the only explanation, but it was certainly one possibility. In light of the John text we do not know whether Jesus believed this or not. It certainly was part of the cultural understanding of the cause of illness. Not only was a physical relationship between sin and sickness assumed, but "sickness and healing were also common metaphors for sin and forgiveness."[9] For those who believed in the physical and causal relationship between sin and sickness or disability, the forgiveness of sin would remove the cause (i.e., sin) which would then remove the punishment (i.e., sickness). One would automatically follow the other.

There is also no denying today that one possible explanation for suffering is that it is a result of our own actions and transgressions. Psychological guilt can produce physical distress, and poor judgment can result in accidents that can cause physical paralysis. "Sin" may or may not be the cause of the guilt or the poor judgment. A man dove off a rock into an unfamiliar lake that was too shallow. His spinal cord was damaged, and he was paralyzed. It was poor judgment, but no one would name it "sin."

When analyzing the relationship between sin and sickness or disability, we see that it is *more* common that symptoms of physical illness and distress manifest themselves in the *victims* of psychological and physical abuse than in the *perpetrators* of such sin. It is true that paralysis, blindness, and deafness can be psychologically induced. However, this

111

type of sensory loss is most often induced not by some sin the person committed, but rather by some atrocious sin committed *against* her or him. What the person saw or heard or experienced was so traumatic that the person cannot cope with the horrible reality of the abuse, and psychological paralysis, blindness, or deafness results. I knew a woman who appeared to be physically deaf and imagined herself to have an inoperable brain tumor—all because she had been physically and sexually abused by her father since the time she was a small child. She could not bear to hear the sounds around her, and she wanted to die. The poet and author Maya Angelou was raped when she was an adolescent, and she named the man who did it. Later, when she witnessed the murder of this man, she felt her words had caused his death, and she could not speak for many years. Psychological paralysis, blindness, deafness, and muteness are ways of coping with the deep pains and traumas people have experienced. It is most often *not* the case that the person committing the sin manifests psychologically induced disability.

The reality today, then, is that there is a relationship between sin and sickness. But, the causal relationship between sin and sickness is that the physical symptoms of illness or disability are sometimes caused by sins that have been committed *against* a person, or possibly by sins a person has committed against himself or herself, as in the case of disability resulting from driving drunk or drugged. It is rare that the physical symptoms of disability are the result of sins committed *by* the person *against* another. To continue to preach that disability is caused by the sins of the person who *has* the disability is to deny both the physical and the psychological causes of disability—namely, sins *against* rather than sins *by* the person with the disability.

Such preaching also perpetuates the cycle of blaming the victim. The one who has been sinned *against* is now ill or disabled. Preaching implicitly or explicitly the cause-and-effect relationship of one's sin and one's illness or disability says the victim is at fault. Since a high percentage of persons who experience disability for psychological reasons are women who have suffered physical and sexual violence, the vicious cycle continues as we assume that the victim deserved the abuse because of some sin she committed. Although the relationship between one's sin and one's sickness was commonly assumed in the first century, we have learned much since then.

To understand the context in which Jesus was operating, it is also important to understand the concept of sin in relation to salvation and how the Greek word *sozein* was used in association with both the healing of the physical body and the healing of the soul—the forgiveness of sins.

> Sin and sickness do come together in Jesus' work; not because one is necessarily the cause of the other, but because he came to save us from both. There is more than one kind of healing, and each kind is called salvation: forgiveness of sins (Luke 7:50; 19:9), psychological healing (as we would call the cleansing of demoniacs; Luke 8:36), and the healing of physical illness. Each involves a different kind of alienation.[10]

Alienation in its various forms separated people from God and from one another. Physical disabilities alienated people from their families, from their social and religious communities, and from their rituals. Because *sozein* was used for the healing of physical illness as well as for the casting out of demons and the forgiveness of sins, the sin/sickness and forgiveness/healing associations were natural at that time. Salvation was both physically and spiritually oriented, and Jesus' ministry involved both.

While it is true that the "forgiveness of sins" section of this text has been used to blame persons with disabilities as the cause of their predicament, this text has also been used by persons within the disability community to discuss the issue of accessibility. When the persons carrying the man with paralysis could not get through the front door of the house, they found an unconventional alternative route of access.

*Verse 1:* The setting of the story is a home in Capernaum in Galilee. Whose home it was is unknown.

*Verse 2:* People came to listen to Jesus. Some were followers, some were curious because word about him had been controversial, and some came to gather more data against him. We learn later that some scribes were among the group that had gathered.

*Verse 3:* The main characters are introduced here. There is a man who is paralyzed to the point that he needs to be carried. Clearly, he is dependent upon others for transportation. We have no knowledge as to how he survived on a daily basis. The text does not say he was a beggar, nor does it say he was still under the care of his family. All it says is that he was accompanied by a group of people. We are not told how many or what their relationship was with the man who is paralyzed. We do know that four of these people were carrying the mat that the man lay on. We do not know what the paralyzed man thought or felt about himself and his life. The people who had gathered would have attributed his paralysis to either his own sin or inherited sin if he had been paralyzed since birth.[11] His physical condition was enough to deny him full status as a member of the Jewish religious community.[12] Most people in his condition were ostracized by the community. So it is curious who the people were who brought him to see Jesus. It is difficult to imagine they were from the religious community of that day. And they probably were not "friends," as is so often described in the commentaries. Most likely they were family members and relatives who believed that blood relations were more important than social codes of behavior. It is fun to imagine, however, that the people accompanying the man with paralysis were just neighbors or members of the religious community who would risk being ostracized in order to befriend this man.

*Verse 4:* When they realized there was no way they would get through the crowd, the people carrying the man became not only persistent but ingenious. They imagined other possibilities for gaining access to Jesus.

This verse is often used by the disability community to support accessibility issues. If a person who is paralyzed cannot get into a church or synagogue because there are steps leading up to the front door, members of the faith community should use their imaginations. Build a ramp or build a door through a side window—whatever works—so that all persons can have access to the place of worship.

In the text, the people "removed the roof" and "dug through it." Roofs in that culture were made of wooden beams that were covered with branches and sealed with mud. Often a stairway to the roof was situated on one of the outside walls.[13] Once the hole was made, the four people lowered the mat on which the man with paralysis lay. The mat was like a stretcher and was a poor man's bed.[14]

What was the man who was paralyzed experiencing? As he lay on his mat, his reality is what he can see above him and what he can hear around him. We do not know whether he was able to move his head from left to right to see what was happening around him. We also do not know if he was able to talk. In this text he does not talk before or after Jesus cures him. As he was lowered into a very crowded room, he was flat on his back, suspended in the air, only able to see the hole in the ceiling, depending totally on the four people not to drop him. Was the man excited about meeting Jesus, or was he embarrassed at the entrance he was making and the commotion he was creating? Had he internalized the belief that his paralysis was his own fault because of some sin he had committed? Did he feel unworthy because of the way people treated him?

*Verse 5:* There are several unique elements in this verse. It says Jesus saw *their* faith. It was not the faith of the person who was paralyzed but the faith of the people who brought him that Jesus recognized. "Faith" here is not a postresurrection understanding of Jesus as divine, but rather "the 'energetic grasping' of the help and power of God."[15] Too often, people with disabilities are told that if they only had enough faith they would be healed. But in this text, it is not the man's faith that was necessary, but the faith of the community of people who cared for this man. It was *their* faith that encouraged Jesus to cure the man. Schweizer says that the "boldness and determination" of the four people who carried him were "more important than a complete knowledge of the person and character of Jesus."[16]

The other unique element of this verse is that this is the only place in a healing narrative where Jesus responds to a request for cure by saying, "your sins are forgiven." Although the request for cure is not a verbal one, the persistent action of those accompanying the man is sufficient to convey their intent. Jesus also calls the man "son," which implies not only a relationship where one is responsible for the other, but also a relationship of belonging, which was often absent from the lives of persons with disabilities.

As was noted earlier, the second part of this verse begins the controversy narrative, which many scholars believe was inserted later into the original story. Note that the last part of verse 10 picks up on the words that end the first part of verse 5: "he said to the paralytic." Verses 1-5a,11-12 read as one whole unit. Verses 5b-10 deal solely with the controversy with the scribes about who has the authority to forgive sins.

*Verses 6-7:* The scribes took Jesus' response as an offense to their traditional beliefs. God alone was able to forgive sins.

This is made clear in Isaiah 43:25, and the "penalty for blasphemy was death by stoning" (Lev. 24:16).[17] In Judaic thought, even the Messiah was not expected to forgive sins.[18]

*Verses 8-9:* Mark informs us that Jesus knew what was in the scribes' hearts and minds and verbally challenged their doubts. He asks, "Which is easier, to say to the paralytic, 'Your sins are forgiven,' or to say 'Stand up and take your mat and walk'?" Putting the controversy story in the middle of the healing narrative creates an unexpected relationship. "Neither in Judaism or Christianity did power to heal imply or infer power to forgive sins."[19] The Greek word *sozein*, however, could be used in both healing and forgiveness of sins. Since the Messiah was not expected to forgive sins, and the power to heal did not infer power to forgive, it is difficult to see how combining the forgiveness of sins with a healing would help prove to the scribes that Jesus was the Messiah.

The connection comes more from the "Son of Man" theology of the postresurrection early church than from Judaism.[20] As a writer to the early Christian community, Mark was addressing their current situation: "The creative *milieu* in which the dialogue took shape is a church which had been charged with blasphemy for dispensing remission of sins in the name of Jesus."[21] The early church was doing both of the things this text deals with—healing persons physically and forgiving sins in the name of Jesus.

*Verse 10:* This verse implies that the healing of the man with paralysis was proof that Jesus had authority on earth to forgive sins. Since healing did not imply power to forgive sins, and given the situation of the early church, it is likely that verse 10 was not said by the earthly Jesus, but was added to the story by the early Christian church.[22]

*Verse 11:* Here, in the climax of Mark's narrative, Jesus tells the man to "stand up, take your mat and go to your home." Here, as in the Bartimaeus text (Mark 10:46-52), Jesus cures with the spoken word only. This was unusual in ancient miracle stories.[23]

*Verse 12:* The image of a man who is totally paralyzed suddenly standing up and walking out with his mat under his arm was much more spectacular than Jesus saying that the man's sins were forgiven, which could not be proved nor demonstrated. The crowds were amazed by the cure that had taken place, because they had never seen anything like it. As a response to what had happened, they glorified God—not Jesus. They believed Jesus' power came from God.

What happened afterward to the man who had been paralyzed is anyone's guess. His thoughts or feelings are never made known to us. Even after he is able to walk, he never says a word. His muscles had not worked for a very long time—possibly for his entire life. Our modern minds presume that the man would have needed a lot of physical therapy along with some job training. But for Mark, the purpose of the healing was to add authority to Jesus' claim to forgive sins, since the early church was continuing to do the same. This combination of narratives also proclaimed once again that Jesus came to alleviate the various conditions that alienated people from God and from one another; it affirmed the same ministry of the early church—to heal both the body and the soul.

## Traditional Homiletic

Because Jesus' ability to forgive sins is more important to Mark and to the early Christian community than is the life of the man who was paralyzed, homileticians tend to focus on the issue of forgiveness as well. Thus, the theology that sin is the cause of the paralysis emerges either implicitly or explicitly.

Homileticians and commentators vary in their approach to this text regarding the focus that should be taken in a sermon. Many encourage preachers to focus on the perceived relationship between sin and sickness, which then requires forgiveness before healing is possible. "There is no sick man healed of his sickness until all his sins have been forgiven," writes William Barclay. "A sick man was a man with whom God was angry."[24] To preach that the reason people get the flu is because God is angry with them, let alone to put forth the notion that once the flu is gone God has forgiven our sins, is beyond absurd.

Although few make such blatant statements as this, a similar notion is prominent in the preaching commentaries on this text. Sin as being the cause of sickness is still emphasized.

> Since sickness manifests the destructive effect of sin, healing and forgiveness are inseparable.[25]

> That sin and suffering are joined in the human condition is the testimony of both Scripture and experience.[26]

> The Bible joins sin and suffering in a more cosmic sense, alienation from God being the root cause of all human woes.[27]

But alienation from God is not the root cause of a person such as Christopher Reeve (a.k.a. Superman) becoming paralyzed from a horseback riding accident. Nor is it the root cause of a child being born blind. But others reiterate this interpretation: "It is not as if this sick man were unusually sinful, but his case . . . illustrates the truth which is proclaimed over and over in the Old Testament, that all suffering is rooted in man's separation from God."[28] Some try to psychologize the issue, but they are still saying the same thing: "[It is] so common to ascribe ills . . . to outward causes

... while all the time the real trouble is sin . . . greed, envy, pride, self-seeking lust."[29]

There are other interpretations of this text, however. Some encourage preachers to focus on the issue of faith. In this text it is the faith of the people who brought the man who was paralyzed to Jesus, not the faith of the man himself. Some believe that faith by *someone* was necessary for the cure to take place.[30] Usually the faith of the person cured is expected, but in this case the faith for healing is found elsewhere. Here attention is often given to the "helplessness of the man," which required "the supreme effort of his friends to bring him to Jesus."[31] The congregation is encouraged to have enough faith for not only the helpless but also the hopeless of our world. This encourages the mistaken common belief that people who are paralyzed are helpless with nothing to offer the community—they only take from those who are strong in their faith and bodies.

Occasionally this text is preached metaphorically. The metaphorical interpretation usually claims that it is not physical paralysis that is the result of sin but a metaphorical notion of paralysis. Sin paralyzes us to act; sin paralyzes our ability to be in healthy relationships with others; sin paralyzes our eagerness to obey God.

## A Healing Homiletic

What other possibilities emerge as we begin to look at the text from the perspective of persons with disabilities? While Jesus does recognize the faith of the people who lowered the man through the roof of the house, he does not say anything out loud about it or require faith before he forgives the man's sins or cures him of his paralysis. Jesus does not place prerequisites on healing. The person who was paralyzed was not required to believe something or even to become a disciple in order for Jesus to cure him. Too often today churches make belief in Jesus Christ a requirement before they will consider a person part of their ministry. Jesus sets no conditions before he brings a healing touch to someone's life.

Jesus' healing ministry was an attempt to break down the walls of alienation that divided the community from its members on the margins. Some people in the disability community feel it would have been better if Jesus had healed the *community* of its common practice of ostracizing all those with disabilities, rather than performing miraculous cures on the persons with disabilities themselves. If the community had been healed in this way, all the people Jesus did not cure back then and now could also become an integral part of the community. But which was easier, curing a few or changing the personal and social attitudes and structures of all? Even today, sometimes it feels like performing a miraculous cure for an individual would be more feasible than changing the social values and negative attitudes of the society at large. Persons with disabilities are still marginalized, perceived as unworthy to be at the center of human relationships and activity. Fighting social structures and attitudes is just too difficult. But since alienation from human relationships is more painful than the physical disability itself, there will not be real healing until the societal structures and attitudes are changed.

In this particular text, Jesus not only cured the man who was paralyzed, he also challenged the systemic structures that perpetuated oppression.[32] The belief that sin was the cause of the paralysis permeated the culture and contributed to the isolation and alienation that persons with disabilities felt. Today we might say that it was a first-century way of blaming the victim. It was a way to make sense of something that could not be explained. By both forgiving the man's sins and curing his paralysis, Jesus broke all the causes of alienation. The man was not only able to walk again, but he was also rid of the stigma that it was his fault; the stigma that made others see him as unworthy; the stigma that made him believe himself to be unworthy all those years.

Today, many churches approach the many social ills of our day with Band-Aid attempts at healing. We have food pantries, we give out Thanksgiving and Christmas baskets, we support Toys for Tots, and we help out in homeless shelters. But the underlying economic, racial, and gendered structures of oppression still exist and are often not dealt with. Addressing physical symptoms of alienation without also addressing the structural and attitudinal forms of alienation that are the root causes does not bring true healing to people's lives.

Dealing head-on with the issue of the relationship between sin and sickness would be another way to approach this text. Instead of the traditional understanding, however, a healing homiletic would focus on the sin *against* a person that results in sickness and suffering rather than the sins committed *by* the person. This is not to deny that there are some cases where the guilt of one's own sin causes suffering or even physical symptoms of illness. But to universalize that as the only explanation of the relationship between sin and sickness continues to blame the victim in most instances. Just to name aloud the reality that many people experience suffering and even psychological paralysis, blindness, or deafness as a result of others' sin *against* them can be a liberating word of hope. An alternative relationship between sin and sickness can be redefined so that barriers of alienation can be broken down.

Another possible way of preaching this text would be to focus on the determination and ingenuity of the people who found an unconventional way to bring someone who was alienated from the religious community to the teaching and healing presence of Jesus. Within the disability community, this is often interpreted as accessibility—making the love of God, the teachings of Jesus, and the healing presence of a faith community accessible to those who are often excluded by architecture and attitude. The attitude that excludes is often shaped by the preaching of these healing narratives and by the theologies espoused in these sermons. A church's architecture usually reflects the attitude (and the pocketbook) of the congregation's leadership and members.

But there are other groups of persons who are likewise alienated and ostracized by faith communities—because of their age, their sexual orientation, their ethnicity or nationality, or their beliefs. With the proper determination, imagination, and ingenuity, what untraditional ways can we envision to bring people to the teaching and healing presence of Jesus? How can we find alternative ways to bring the teaching and healing presence of Jesus to those on the margins?

# CHAPTER SIX

# Leprosy and Chronic Illness

While many of the Gospel healing narratives describe the healing of those who were blind, deaf, paralyzed (lame), and mute to show how Jesus fulfills the eschatological proclamation in Isaiah 35:5-6, the Gospels also describe the healing of those who were "possessed by demons"[1] and those who were considered "unclean." Although none of these persons (except for the boy with epilepsy in Luke 9:37-43a; Mark 9:14-29; Matt. 17:14-21) had a physical disability per se, each of them was still included in Jesus' healing ministry. The most familiar accounts of Jesus healing those who were identified as "unclean" are those that describe Jesus' cleansing of persons with leprosy. But, as Donald Gowan notes, the persons with leprosy fit into a broad category of people who are ostracized by the community:

> As people considered to be unclean they [persons with leprosy] are classic examples of alienation, in the New Testament, and so they fit the traditional list of disabilities, once we recognize the prophets chose those people for attention because they are regularly left out of participation in the life of their community. Several of the other healing stories may now be seen to fit the pattern. The woman who had suffered from a hemorrhage for twelve years had been ritually unclean for that whole time.[2]

There are a few stories about the cleansing of persons with leprosy in general (Matt. 10:8, 11:5; Luke 7:22), and Simon is known to be a "leper" (Matt. 26:6 and Mark 14:3), but there are only two specific stories of leprosy in the Gospels: the cleansing of the one person with leprosy, in Mark 1:40-45 (with parallels in Matt. 8:1-4 and Luke 5:12-14); and the cleansing of the ten persons with leprosy, in Luke 17:11-19. Both are included in the Revised Common Lectionary. In addition to the leprosy texts, the lectionary includes one other pericope that deals with ritual impurity: the healing of the woman with the flow of blood, in Mark 5:25-34 (also Matt. 9:20-22 and Luke 8:43-48).[3]

## Ritual Purity Laws

Concepts of "clean" and "unclean" were part of the ritual purity codes found in Leviticus 11-17 and Numbers 19. These purity laws dealt with a variety of situations that would cause people and things to be considered "unclean," and they prohibited such persons or things from having any contact with the Temple. Uncleanness or impurity was seen as a threat to holiness, and hence was to be kept separate from the Temple, which housed the presence of God.[4] Ritual purity laws reflect the belief that God might withdraw from the Temple if the Temple were to become polluted by unclean people or things. Since other religions had their own purity codes, the ritual purity laws of Leviticus applied only to Jews, not to Gentiles.[5]

An explicit rationale for the purity codes is not given in the Torah.[6] However, "it is certain that the rabbis did not regard the impurities as infectious diseases or the laws of purification as quasi-hygienic principles, for otherwise they would not have excluded Gentiles from various impurities."[7] The theological rationale is assumed to be Leviticus 11:44-45, in which God says, "Be holy, for I am holy"; for it is immediately following this verse that the causes for impurity are delineated and the purification rites are given. Some scholars believe that the body was a symbol for the larger community. The body had its own orifices that symbolized holes or breaks in the boundaries of the body. The mouth orifice symbolized what clean and unclean foods could enter the body. Childbirth, menstruation, and bodily discharges from the genitals caused a person to be "unclean"; and leprosy was a sign that the boundaries of the body (the skin) or the boundaries of walls (mildew or fungus) were being invaded.[8] Purity codes that protected others from invasions of the boundaries of the body were representative of the protection desired against invasions of the boundaries of the community's religious and social life.[9]

While the rationale for purity laws is still being debated, the causes of ritual impurity are made clear in Leviticus. The *Encyclopaedia Judaica Jerusalem* delineates them as "leprosy, issue from human sexual organs, and the dead bodies of certain animals, and particularly human corpses."[10] Some of these causes, such as bodily discharges, were natural. Others, however, were considered to be impure because of sinful behaviors or situations. Leprosy, like other disabilities, was considered a punishment for some sin or transgression the person had committed (see 2 Chron. 26:16-21; 2 Kings 5:15-27).

The state of impurity was separate from the physical condition itself, and therefore impurity could be passed on from one person to another, from one person to an object, or from an object to a person. It was not a physical contagion but rather the *state of impurity* that was passed on. Since walls and other objects that contained fungal matter could be considered leprous, an object, as well as a person, could be the cause of impurity.

The initial impurity was called the "father of impurity." Persons who came in contact with this "father of impurity"

126

would also be considered unclean, and even though this "second generation" did not manifest any of the physical symptoms of the "father of impurity," they could also transfer the state of uncleanness to others. This chain of transference usually occurred for only two or three generations, so that the impurity was not passed on ad infinitum. "Only in the case of sexual intercourse with a menstruant (or, deductively, with a woman in the first stage of impurity after childbirth or a woman with an abnormal sexual flow) is there a chain four generations long."[11]

There were two types of impurity: communicable and noncommunicable. Communicable forms of impurity could pollute both the holy sphere and the nonholy (profane) sphere of community life. Some form of quarantine—restriction from contact with other people as well as with the Temple—was required for those in this category. Noncommunicable forms of impurity polluted only the holy sphere. Like those with communicable forms of impurity, those with noncommunicable forms were excluded from the Temple, but they could wander through the town and be accepted on the Temple grounds outside the sanctuary, in the "habitation" area.

Purification rituals were the only means of rectifying the impure state of being. How long the impurity lasted and what rituals were required depended on the kind of impurity and its degree. The mildest form of impurity lasted "until the evening following contraction of the impurity."[12] The greater degrees of impurity lasted for seven days. However, the three texts included in the lectionary deal with degrees of impurity that were exceptions to the general rule. For persons with leprosy and men or women who had abnormal flows from sexual organs, the state of impurity lasted until the condition was gone.[13] Even then, a seven-day waiting period was required, to be sure it did not come back. At the end of the unclean period, washing or bathing was required of the person and the objects that had been polluted. Earthenware vessels, stoves, and ovens, however, could not be purified; they had to be broken.[14]

Since being in a state of impurity excluded all such persons from the religious life of the community, and for those with communicable impurities, the social life and family life as well, it was a tremendously isolating experience. It was made worse by the common belief that "the state of impurity [was] considered hateful to God."[15]

Jesus clearly was familiar with the Leviticus purity laws. However, he also was influenced by Hellenistic purity codes and by the understanding of purity and impurity that was practiced by the Qumran community.[16] In Qumran, clean and unclean referred to those who joined the community and either followed or ignored the ethical precepts and cultic practices of Qumran rather than to those who embodied the physical conditions of impurity outlined in Leviticus. Those who were faithful members of the community were "clean" or "pure," and those who were not faithful members were "unclean" or "impure."[17]

Jesus' teaching and ministry began to challenge the traditional purity laws and shifted the concept of pure and impure from the physical realm to the ethical realm. Mark 7:14-23 is a classic example of Jesus challenging the laws that declared foods clean or unclean and moving the discussion to a notion of purity as that which comes from one's heart as it pertains to one's right relationships with others. When Jesus ate with tax collectors and sinners, when he came in contact with Lazarus (who was considered dead), when he touched persons with leprosy, and when he was willing to be touched by the woman with the flow of blood, he challenged the purity codes that declared people "unclean."

## Leprosy in Biblical Times

Today, leprosy is called Hansen's disease. It is clear that Hansen's disease, or true leprosy, is not what is meant in the Leviticus texts. But it is possible that, by the time of Jesus, Hansen's disease could have been one of many diseases that identified a person as having leprosy. A basic translation of the Hebrew term *sara'at* and the Greek word *lepra* is "a repulsive, scaly skin disease."[18] In the Hebrew Bible, *sara'at* could refer to people, fabrics, or walls of houses. In the New Testament, *lepra* was limited to various human skin diseases. What we currently know as psoriasis, eczema, and seborrhea would have been identified as leprosy in biblical times.

Today, we would not consider a case of psoriasis cause for ostracizing a person from the community and labeling them ritually unclean. Hansen's disease is another matter, however. Persons who have true leprosy are still shunned and avoided. This response stems partly from the stories of "leper colonies" and the belief that it is a highly contagious disease, and partly from the negative connotations that surround leprosy in the biblical texts.

We now know more about what causes the disease, and while treatment is crucial, isolation of patients is not necessary. There are over 5.5 million persons with Hansen's disease worldwide, but fewer than two hundred new cases per year are found in the United States, most of which are identified in recent immigrants.[19] While many of us do not know a single person with leprosy, those who live with this disease still experience tremendous isolation and ostracism from religious communities and society at large because of the attitudes that have been formed by these biblical texts and purity laws.

The ritual purity codes concerning persons with leprosy are found in Leviticus 13:1-46 and 14:1-32. Leprosy was considered the first of the "fathers of impurity." It was an initial impurity that could cause others to likewise become impure. It was not the case that the disease was considered contagious. The disease itself was not passed on, only the condition or state of being impure.

Because leprosy was not only a "father of impurity" but also a communicable form of impurity, there were many restrictions placed on persons with leprosy. Not only were they barred from the Temple, but they were also excluded from the habitation area that surrounded the tent of meeting or Temple. They were supposed to live alone, outside the camp (Lev. 13:46), away from their families and friends. As a sign of their leprous and "unclean" condition, their clothes were to be torn and their hair kept disheveled. They were to cover their upper lip and cry "unclean, unclean" whenever they were in the presence of others for as long as their condition continued and they were deemed "unclean."

If the symptoms of the disease disappeared, the priest would perform the purification ritual, which involved two living birds, hyssop, cedar wood, and crimson yarn (Lev. 14:4). One of the birds was killed over fresh water in an earthen vessel (v. 5), then the yarn, hyssop, and living bird were dipped in the blood of the slaughtered bird (v. 6). The blood was sprinkled on the person with leprosy seven times, after which the living bird was set free as a sign of the release of the person from the state of impurity.

Once this had been done, the person was to wash all his or her clothes, shave the hair on his or her head, and bathe in water (Lev. 14:8). The person was then allowed to move about in the camp, but was not allowed inside the tent or the Temple for another seven days (v. 8). At the end of the seven-day waiting period, the person was to shave all his or her hair, including any facial hair, and wash his or her clothes and body again (v. 9). On the eighth day, animal, grain, and oil offerings were made; and the purification ritual was completed (v. 10). Now pronounced clean, the person could resume full membership within the community.

By the time of Jesus, people with leprosy were gathering in and around the populated regions in hopes of collecting alms. Having no employment, no place to live, and the ability to defile not only the sacral life of the community but its daily functioning as well, persons with leprosy lived in isolation and poverty. In the Markan narrative, the man with leprosy appears to be alone.

The Text
**Mark 1:40-45**

> [40] A leper came to him begging him, and kneeling he said to him, "If you choose, you can make me clean." [41]Moved with pity, Jesus stretched out his hand and touched him, and said to him, "I do choose. Be made clean!" [42]Immediately the leprosy left him, and he was made clean. [43]After sternly warning him he sent him away at once, [44]saying to him, "See that you say nothing to anyone; but go, show yourself to the priest, and offer for your cleansing what Moses commanded, as a testimony to them." [45]But he went out and began to proclaim it freely, and to spread the word, so that Jesus could no longer go into a town openly, but stayed out in the country; and people came to him from every quarter.

# Hermeneutics

Most scholars believe this text is a basic healing narrative that focuses on the words and actions of Jesus:[20] the person with leprosy requests to be made clean, Jesus responds with a word and a touch, and the leprosy leaves him. It is a short and straightforward story. The most unusual aspect of this text is found in verses 41 and 43, where anger is evoked on the part of Jesus. Anger is an emotion seldom used in the Gospels in relation to Jesus and is not found in any of the other healing narratives. The story comes after Jesus has already cast out unclean spirits and healed many people, and begins the conflict section of Mark's Gospel.

Verse 39 tells us that Jesus is traveling throughout Galilee "proclaiming the message in the synagogues and casting out demons."[21] It is here in Galilee that the story begins. Jesus is approached by a man who has leprosy. Will Jesus observe the proper behavior in relationship to persons labeled "unclean" or will he challenge these norms and be lax about obedience to the purity codes?

*Verse 40:* The person with leprosy approaches Jesus and kneels in front of him. The person does not keep his proper distance from Jesus, nor does he shout "unclean, unclean." Instead he comes right up to Jesus and addresses him directly. He knows Jesus is not a priest and that by approaching him he is violating the purity laws. But sheer desperation may be motivating him to disregard the law and seek help no matter what the cost. After all, what more can the community do to him? Or perhaps the man has heard that Jesus is flexible when it comes to the purity laws and has violated some of them himself by touching those who are considered unclean. Or, though faith is not mentioned in the text at all, perhaps some faith in Jesus' abilities has given him the impetus to confront Jesus. For whatever reason, the man with leprosy disobeys the rules, goes to Jesus directly, and asks Jesus to do something that Jesus has no legal authority to do—pronounce the man clean. Only a priest can do that.

Kneeling, he says to Jesus, "If you choose, you can make me clean." This is the only healing narrative in which the person gives Jesus a choice. The man with leprosy knows that he is asking Jesus to break the religious law, so he gives Jesus a chance to refuse. He does not demand anything from Jesus. He recognizes Jesus' ability but leaves the decision up to him. He does not ask to be cured or healed of his disease, but rather he asks to be cleansed, to be labeled "clean" so that he can return to his family and the rest of the community as a full member. The disease itself is not so bad, but the social ostracism that results from being perceived as a threat to the purity of the community is unbearable. He wants the stigma removed so that he can once again be in relationship with his friends and family.

This is true of many persons with disabilities today. They could deal with and adapt to the disability itself, if only the stigma and social ostracism would be removed.

*Verses 41 and 43:* It is here (in verse 41) that conflict arises between the words *orgistheis* ("was angered") and *splagchnizesthai* ("to be moved with compassion or pity," "to feel sympathy," "to have one's bowels yearn"). Ancient readings use *orgistheis*, which is consonant with *embrimaomai* ("to snort with anger," "to have indignation on," "to blame," "to murmur against," "to groan") in verse 43. But more recently discovered manuscripts use *splagchnizesthai*, which arouses a deep sense of compassion, in contrast to the anger and indignation described in verse 43 with the use of *embrimaomai*. If one chooses the compassionate wording of this verse, one still has to face the anger found in verse 43, even though the New Revised Standard Version translates *embrimaomai* as "sternly warning." What was Jesus angry about?

Scholars pose various reasons for Jesus' anger: It is "anger against the symbolic order of purity of which this man is a victim."[22] Or "Jesus is moved by anger because he recognizes the leprosy to be a manifestation of evil; the sick man brings him face to face with the powers of evil."[23] Another rationale is that Jesus is angry at the man's bold approach, which was forbidden to a person with leprosy, and at his impetuous demand.[24] But it is clear from verse 40 that the man's request is anything but a demand, since he gives Jesus a choice. Another scholar poses the argument that Jesus becomes angry "because of the blindness of the man who praises the miracle-worker but wants nothing to do with his cross."[25] This interpretation not only uses blindness metaphorically and negatively, but also makes a negative judgment on the man whom Jesus heals, based on no textual evidence. Another scholar says, "The anger was provoked by the situation or by the sight of leprosy but not directed against the leper himself."[26] Still another believes that "Jesus' pity is not the reason for this healing. The reason is to be found in the far more comprehensive campaign which is waged against every ungodly thing and in which the special authority of Jesus is revealed."[27] And it is possible that Jesus was simply angry at the misery caused, not so much by the disease itself, but by the laws that labeled people with the disease unclean.

Whether through anger at the religious system that kept the person with leprosy ostracized or through anger at diseases that thwart God's good creation, Jesus reaches through the man's alienation and chooses to make him clean. He also chooses to touch him. With this choice, Jesus defies Torah and places himself in the role of priestly authority.

In this narrative, Jesus heals with both the spoken word and a physical touch, which is somewhat unusual. This combination is found in only two other places: Mark 5:41, in which Jesus touches the daughter of the synagogue leader as he raises her from her deathbed; and Mark 7:33, in which Jesus touches the deaf man's ears. In this one touch, Jesus accepts the man and creates a new vision of a compassionate community that includes those who have been considered outside the boundaries.

By touching the man, Jesus himself becomes polluted and "unclean" according to the purity laws. But Mark tells us that instead of Jesus becoming "unclean" and unacceptable, the man with leprosy becomes clean and accepted. Jesus' act of touching a person with leprosy would have been the most shocking element of the incident for the people in that culture. "To concentrate on the cure-miracle aspect is to miss this basic cultural dynamic which, we would argue, is the central concern of this part of the story in Mark."[28]

*Verse 42:* We are told that the leprosy leaves the man immediately and that he is made clean. We do not know what form of biblical leprosy the man suffered from, so we do not know what physical changes occurred in him. But we do know that being "clean" had enormous religious, social, and cultural implications for his life.

*Verse 44:* In traditional Markan style, Jesus tells the man "to *say nothing* to anyone," but to "go, show yourself to the priest, and offer for your cleansing what Moses commanded, as a testimony to them." Jesus violates the purity laws by touching the person with leprosy; then he sends the man to the priest in order to fulfill the purification requirements established by the same laws Jesus has just broken. It seems contradictory, and yet the combination of both breaking and fulfilling the law was consonant with much of Jesus' ministry. The text might be intended to show that Jesus respects· the priests and the Mosaic law even while he challenges their negative effects on humanity; or it might be offered as a recognition that in the midst of transforming society, " 'unofficial limit breakers' nevertheless [have to] abide by the precepts of the officials who preside over the ceremonial life of the nation."[29] Jesus was caught between a new vision of community and the "real" world out there, to which the man had to return.

The offering the man would be asked to make would be that which is outlined in detail in Leviticus 13–14. Once he saw the priest, he would still have to wait seven more days before he would be considered ritually clean.

Jesus warns the man not to tell anyone about what happened—but the clearing up of one's skin disease is not something that can be hidden. It is not the cure itself, but rather the encounter itself—particularly the touch—that Jesus does not want people to know about. Jesus' reason for commanding the man not to tell anyone is probably not his fear of publicity concerning the cure (as is often the explanation for Jesus' secrecy in the Gospel of Mark), but rather that if the religious community learned of this encounter Jesus would be considered unclean as well. The "cleansed leper's task is not to publicize a miracle but to help confront an ideological system."[30] In confronting the system, Jesus puts himself at risk, which becomes even more clear in verse 45.

*Verse 45:* Mark tells us that instead of obeying Jesus' command, the man does not go directly to the priest, but instead "went out and began to proclaim it freely." He starts preaching. The result of this is that "Jesus could no longer go into a town openly, but stayed out in the country." Contact with a person with leprosy requires Jesus to also be in a state of impurity. Once the people learn of Jesus' actions, he too is shunned and considered "unclean." No longer welcome in the town, he retreats to the countryside. There are some, however, "from every quarter," who are attracted to Jesus' unconventional but compassionate behavior and seek Jesus out in the countryside.

# Traditional Homiletic

Today, we need to recognize that there are still persons among us who have Hansen's disease. Although they are few in number, we should not make them invisible or shun them because of our attitudes based on biblical notions of impurity. Of course, there are many more who have skin diseases that would have been identified as leprosy in biblical times, but our modern minds would not think of ostracizing persons because they have psoriasis or eczema. When deciding how to preach the healing texts, most preachers are even less likely to consider actual people with Hansen's disease than they are to consider people who are blind, deaf, or paralyzed. Those who have Hansen's disease need not be the focus of our sermons, but their existence in our world should be remembered.

Traditionally, sin and faith have been common themes found in sermons on this text. Though neither term appears in the text, the presence both of sin and faith in the man with leprosy is often preached. Faith is usually understood as a necessary requirement for any healing, and it appears in the homiletical suggestions for this text as well.[31] Sin receives even more attention in the literature: "Leprosy symbolizes sin";[32] "Like sin it is contagious."[33] But leprosy was not contagious, nor was it a sinful state; rather, it was a state of impurity.

Instead of focusing on the connection between sin and leprosy—either as being in a cause and effect relationship or as leprosy being a sinful state—some scholars attribute the leprosy to demon possession, which is not even alluded to in the text: the "leper is a demoniac plagued by an unclean spirit"[34]; "Jesus dismissed the demon that caused the leprosy."[35] But demon possession in relationship to leprosy is not a common biblical theme. Leprosy was a case of impurity.

In recent years, the concept of leprosy has been applied to another group of persons who are deemed "unclean" or untouchable by society and the church: those with the HIV and AIDS. The connection between having HIV and AIDS and being labeled "unclean" in our society is a reality. Persons living with HIV and AIDS are no more unclean than the rest of us, but they are treated as such by people who prejudge them because of their disease.

As preachers, we must be mindful of the terminology we use as we educate our congregations about persons with HIV and AIDS. It is unfortunate but true that our society often perceives persons with HIV and AIDS as "modern-day lepers," because of the current unwritten purity codes that label persons "unclean" or "impure." If true leprosy (or deafness or blindness for that matter) were no longer around, the word "leper" would have only historical or metaphorical meaning. But there are still persons today who live with Hansen's disease, and many more with various skin diseases that were labeled leprous in biblical times. The use of the word "leper" in relation to persons with HIV and AIDS not only is degrading to those with HIV and AIDS, but also perpetuates the notion that people with Hansen's disease are unclean, contagious outcasts. Since "leper" and "leprosy" have such negative connotations, persons today who have Hansen's disease should not be labeled "lepers" either.

When preaching against the inaccurate, unjust, and ill-informed perceptions that stigmatize persons with HIV and AIDS, it is safest to use "unclean" as the metaphor rather than "leprosy" or "leper" in describing how society draws boundaries around those it considers acceptable and unacceptable.

# A Healing Homiletic

What other possibilities emerge as we reconsider this text? We can focus on our own "purity codes"—those unwritten religious and societal rules that identify those who are within the accepted boundaries and those who are outside. Socially, the boundaries are often divided along economic and racial lines. Within the religious realm, the boundaries are drawn by moral standards. The church decides what is unholy and therefore what is displeasing to God, and rejects those who fit this definition. Sin is also defined by faith communities, and those considered living in sin are "unclean" and "impure" and not acceptable to the holy realm. Though we may mock the ancient, written laws defining what is clean and unclean, we have our own unwritten purity codes that we live by. But keeping people outside the boundaries creates desperate situations in peoples' lives. Ostracized and feeling hopeless, those relegated to the outer margins of society have nothing to lose.

Jesus, however, did not abide by the established social or religious boundaries. He reached out and touched the man with leprosy. By so doing he challenged the norms and established a new code of compassion. He constantly went outside the boundaries to welcome people back into the center of community life.[36] His actions were not without cost; he risked being identified as "unclean" himself and therefore risked being rejected by the community. But Jesus was willing to accept the consequences in order to reach out and effect a change in the man's self-identity as well as in his personal and religious relationships.

When we do reach out beyond the established conventional boundaries, people are changed and we are transformed as well. New relationships foster new definitions of the self. "Jesus' 'cure' invariably involved establishing new self-understandings so that those formerly 'unclean' and excluded from the holy community now found themselves 'clean' and within the holy community."[37] Rejection is transformed to acceptance, exclusion to inclusion, alienation and isolation to fostering relationships, and hopelessness to proclamation.

Today, persons outside the boundaries (including persons with disabilities) are challenging the unwritten symbolic codes established by faith communities that label certain behaviors as sinful and some states of being (for example, homelessness) as "unclean" and therefore not fit for the holy sphere. Sin and impurity are still functioning as rationales behind our own unwritten purity codes. Persons with disabilities are often placed outside the boundaries because of the underlying notion that disability is caused by sin, or because of the belief that persons with disabilities are somehow not whole and therefore not holy. People within the church may believe that such obvious lack of wholeness is a sign of sin or at least is displeasing to God and therefore not appropriate in the holy sanctuary or among the holy people who worship there. Underlying purity codes do exist within our congregations, and persons with disabilities and other "outsiders" are approaching and making their wishes known: they want to be included in the community. Like the man with leprosy in the story, most are giving churches a choice—"if you choose." Unfortunately, unlike Jesus, many churches are choosing to say no. Whether the fear is defilement, or the risk is simply too great, boundaries are maintained, and persons are kept on the outside. However, by choosing to say yes, we can bring a healing touch of respect, acceptance, and affirmation to people's lives.

LEPROSY AND CHRONIC ILLNESS

The Text
**Luke 17:11-19**

> $^{11}$"On the way to Jerusalem Jesus was going through the region between Samaria and Galilee. $^{12}$As he entered a village, ten lepers approached him. Keeping their distance, $^{13}$they called out, saying, "Jesus, Master, have mercy on us!" $^{14}$When he saw them, he said to them, "Go and show yourselves to the priests." And as they went, they were made clean. $^{15}$Then one of them, when he saw that he was healed, turned back, praising God with a loud voice. $^{16}$He prostrated himself at Jesus' feet and thanked him. And he was a Samaritan. $^{17}$Then Jesus asked, "Were not ten made clean? But the other nine, where are they? $^{18}$Was none of them found to return and give praise to God except this foreigner?" $^{19}$Then he said to him, "Get up and go on your way; your faith has made you well."

## *Hermeneutics*

The story of the ten persons with leprosy is found only in the Gospel of Luke and is believed to be Luke's variation on Mark's narrative of the cleansing of the person with leprosy (Mark 1:40-45), discussed above. Luke has added so much of his own perspective to Mark's version that some scholars believe that "Luke is the author of the whole narrative."[38]

Most agree that at least verses 11 and 19 were composed and added by Luke. In effect, Luke's version turns a miracle story into a pronouncement story. The focus of the text moves from the miracle of the healing of the ten persons with leprosy (vv. 11-14) to the issue of praise and thanksgiving, which is evoked by Jesus' rhetorical questions: "Were not ten made clean? But the other nine, where are they? Was none of them found to return and give praise to God except this foreigner?" (vv. 15-18). Unlike most miracle stories, which focus on the situation of those in need and on how the miracle worker effects the cure, this text emphasizes the pronouncement verses over the cleansing of the ten persons with leprosy.[39]

This narrative makes a comparison between the nine Jews and the one Gentile Samaritan. This is understandable, because Luke himself was a Gentile and was writing to a Gentile community. It was important to have Gentiles as models of faith for the new Christian community. The narrative about the cleansing of ten persons with leprosy, then, becomes a missionary story, for it is the Gentile who is honored by Jesus for giving praise to God.[40] Luke utilized the Naaman text from 2 Kings 5 as the basis for this narrative. Naaman had leprosy, and he was also a foreigner. But once he was cured, he returned to give thanks and became converted and worshiped the God of Israel. The Samaritan, likewise, is a foreigner and shows his faith by returning to give thanks and praise. Both the Naaman story and this text are concerned more with the conversion experience than with the cleansing itself.[41] In the Luke text, the healing does not even take place in the presence of Jesus, but rather while the ten persons with leprosy are on their way to the priests. Curing at a distance is very unusual in the healing narratives.

It is clear in Jewish law that Gentiles were not obliged to obey the Leviticus purity codes.[42] Therefore, sending a Gentile to a Jewish priest to be pronounced clean and to follow through on the purification rituals prescribed by Jewish law would be inappropriate.

It was also inappropriate for Jews to associate with Samaritans at all, so it is uncommon to find a group of persons with leprosy that includes both Jews and Samaritans. But clearly the common condition of being ostracized by family and society was enough to break down whatever religious barriers existed between them.

*Verse 11:* According to Luke, Jesus has been on his way to Jerusalem since chapter 9:51. En route, he passes through the region between Samaria and Galilee and is confronted by the ten people with leprosy.

*Verse 12:* By the first century, persons with leprosy were traveling in groups on the outskirts of populated areas in hopes of receiving alms from the members of the community.

*Verse 13:* Like Bartimaeus, the lepers cry out, "Jesus, have mercy on us!" However, instead of addressing Jesus as "Son of David" as Bartimaeus does, they address Jesus as "Master." The address "Master," however, does not carry christological inferences. It could mean "teacher," or anyone with more authority than the persons with leprosy. The cry for mercy may simply be a "request for human compassion and momentary fellowship"[43] or a request for alms. The persons with leprosy do not explicitly request cleansing or cure. Jesus does not ask the persons with the illness what they want from him, as he does in the Bartimaeus text. He has no conversation with them at all.

*Verse 14:* When Jesus sees who is calling out to him, he commands them to "go and show yourselves to the priests." In contrast to his actions in the Mark 1:40-45 text, Jesus does not overtly break the law and touch any of the persons with leprosy. He does not risk becoming "unclean" himself. However, Jesus speaks as if they already are cured of whatever disease has caused them to become impure. Jesus commands them to show themselves to the priests before any visible cure of the disease has taken place. What would the persons with leprosy be thinking? They can see that their skin is no different, and yet they start off on their way to see the priests. It is difficult to believe they would expect some cure to happen to them once they leave Jesus' presence. Curing from a distance, as well as effecting a cure without any words, gestures, or physical elements, was very uncommon. Jesus does not send them off with any instructions (for example, to wash in the pool or dip seven times in the river as Naaman did) that would imply they would be cured once they followed the instructions. And yet they obey Jesus' command to go and show themselves to the priests. Some scholars identify their willingness to go—skin diseases and all—as faith. As they were walking along, they were made clean.

*Verse 15:* The Samaritan in the group sees that he is cured and goes back praising God. As a Samaritan, going to the Jewish priests would be foolish anyway. He does not have to perform any purification rites according to the Leviticus laws. He is free to go wherever he chooses. It is here, however, that the conversion takes place. The Samaritan realizes it is the power of God that has cured him. Once he sees that his disease is gone, he praises God. The Greek word for praise, *doxazo*, can also mean "to glorify, to magnify, to honor" and is the origin of our liturgical term "doxology."

*Verse 16:* In this verse we first learn that the person who has returned to give thanks is a Samaritan—a foreigner and a Gentile. He prostrates himself at Jesus' feet and thanks him. It is from the Greek word for thanks, *eucharisteo*, that we derive our word "Eucharist."

*Verses 17-18:* The healing scene is exceptionally brief in order for the narrative to build to the pronouncement in these two verses. Jesus asks where the other nine are and why only the foreigner has returned to give praise to God. But the other nine are only doing what Jesus has commanded them and what the law of Moses requires of them in order to be accepted back into the community. Until they are pronounced clean they are still able to pollute Jesus and everyone else who comes in contact with them. The Samaritan is not bound by the same laws and is free to go back to Jesus. But Luke wants to set Gentiles up as role models of faith—to show that new converts have faith equal to or greater than those who have inherited the tradition of belief in the one God, Yahweh.

*Verse 19:* This closing verse is a Lukan addition that relates the Samaritan's praise and thanksgiving to faith and salvation. "Your faith has made you well" may be better translated, "Your faith has made you whole." Faith had not been required before the cure could take place. The cure is a gift without price and comes long before the man acknowledges and praises God. But now that the man believes, his newfound faith brings a sense of "wholeness" to his life. While he is still prostrated at Jesus' feet, Jesus tells the man to "get up and go on your way."

## *Traditional Homiletic*

Preachers often compare and contrast gratitude and ingratitude when preaching this text, emphasizing that we should always remember to give thanks to Jesus: "The ingratitude was a worse leprosy than the physical disease";[44] or, we have a "tendency merely to do what is necessary to get what we need for life without ever bothering to stop and give rightful thanks to God for all life's blessings."[45] It is true that the Samaritan comes back and thanks Jesus. But Jesus' response to him is not, "Why did not the other nine return and thank me?" but rather, "Was none of them found to return and give praise to God except this foreigner?" Jesus is not looking for praise or thanks for himself. Jesus is not recognizing a personalized thank-you card. Jesus is honoring the man's newfound heart-knowledge of the God of Israel—his ability to praise, to give honor and glory to God for God's presence in his life.

Another common theme homileticians stress is that of the importance of worship in addition to obedience: "Mere obedience without grateful worship is insufficient."[46] The implication is that the nine Jews are simply obeying Jesus' command and do not worship God. But in obeying Jesus and going to the priests, the Jews would participate in the purification ritual, which involved making offering to God in worship. Worship would occur, but in a different context.

For Luke, the contrast between the faith of the Gentile Samaritan and that of the other nine is important, but the truth is that we do not know whether the Jewish persons with leprosy do or do not praise God as they make their way to the priests and notice their own skin diseases have disappeared. It is hard to believe that they, too, do not rejoice as they obey Jesus' command to show themselves to the priests.

But what if their rejoicing is simply out of relief that the ordeal is over? What if they decide that it is too painful to praise God for their cure when the laws given by the same God are what has made them unclean in the first place? What if they cry tears of relief that their living death is finally over? Religious ostracism and exclusion often has a negative effect on people's faith. It gives a clear message that they are not acceptable to God and therefore God does not love them. We exclude certain people from our churches, then judge these same people because they do not have faith—because they do not give praise and thanks to God. Why should they, if

146

God does not love them? The church sends out double messages. We often do not welcome or accept persons with disabilities into our faith communities, and yet we expect them to have faith enough to be healed, or faith enough to sustain them in their struggles, or at least the ability to give thanks to God for what they do have. We set up barriers to faith for persons living with HIV and AIDS, for those who are addicted to drugs or alcohol, for persons living on the streets who have no home, and for anyone else we deem to be "unclean" in our society. But then we judge them for their lack of faith or simply write them off as unredeemable.

## A Healing Homiletic

It is the outsider in the text whose faith is praised by Jesus, the one least expected to praise God, the one doubly ostracized because of his disease and his being a Gentile among Jews. It is this message that was close to the heart of Luke, as he was preaching to people whose newfound faith in God was suspect because they were Gentiles. What do outsiders have to teach us today? What lessons do those considered "foreigners" among us have to offer? What can we learn from the faith of those considered "unclean" or "impure"?

Luke's narrative has clearly shifted the focus of the pericope from the cleansing of ten persons with leprosy to the conversion of a Gentile Samaritan. But the healing aspect of the story should not be forgotten. Once again, Jesus responds to those who are ostracized by society and enables them in their own way to re-enter the community. The Jews he sends to the priests to fulfill the purification rite in order to be pronounced "clean," and the Samaritan he sends on his way.

The narrative also tends to focus on the Samaritan and all but dismisses the other nine. But the nine are also important in this text. From the very beginning, we know that they have chosen to disregard their religious norm of not associating

147

with Samaritans. They have included the Samaritan among them. They have chosen not to ostracize him because he is a foreigner and a Gentile. The Jewish persons with leprosy have intentionally broken down barriers and challenged cultural and religious norms in order to include the Samaritan man in their group. Putting aside differences as we join together in the struggle and sometimes the sufferings of life is an important lesson the nine have to offer us. Crossing racial and religious lines that divide us in order to be in solidarity with one another may relieve the isolation so many people feel in our world today.

The third text included in the lectionary that deals with ritual impurity is the story of the woman who has been bleeding for twelve years. Her condition makes her "unclean" in the same way that the persons with leprosy are "unclean." While I recognize this perception of "uncleanness" as an important element in the text, I want to concentrate on another aspect of the text. This woman represents many persons who live much of their lives with illnesses that will not go away. Today, medical conditions that cannot be cured and that continue for long periods of time are known as chronic illnesses.

## Chronic Illness

Chronic illnesses are varied. Included among chronic illnesses are arthritis, cancer, the dementias, diabetes, the epilepsies, heart disease, respiratory diseases, strokes, substance addiction, multiple sclerosis, sickle cell anemia, AIDS, and other more rare, less prevalent diseases.[47]

Nearly every congregation in the country has members who live with some kind of chronic illness. As the list of chronic illnesses demonstrates, each of these diseases is unique and has its own ramifications, but chronic illnesses do have several things in common. Some people are born with the disease or contract it early in childhood. Living with the disease becomes a natural part of who they are. Those who contract the disease in adulthood relate to the disease in different ways. Some are in total denial, while others recognize the disease within themselves but hide it from everyone else. When first diagnosed with a chronic illness, the person and his or her loved ones sometimes become very desperate, knowing there is little or no chance of being cured. As time goes on, some make the disease a part of their identity, and others almost become the illness as their lives are totally determined by it.[48] However the disease becomes integrated into one's identity, self-esteem is almost always affected as one learns how to manage the disease.

Most people who are chronically ill experience feelings of powerlessness, loss of control, and isolation. The lack of predictability can also be extremely frustrating. The reality is that many persons with chronic illness can no longer depend on their bodies. Some feel as if they cannot trust their bodies or as if their bodies have betrayed them, while others see their bodies as alien entities.[49] Energy levels, muscle strength, endurance, and the ability to get from one place to another are all unpredictable from one minute to the next. For some diseases, the periods of remission are days or months, sometimes even years, but for others, the periods of "remission" are just a few minutes or hours. Not knowing how one will feel at any given moment is very frustrating.

To maintain one's physical functioning and to reduce the risk of making things worse, a tight daily regimen—involving diet, exercise, medication, sleep, and periods of rest—is required of almost all persons with chronic illnesses. Following such a structured regimen often means reducing other activities. However, too much reduced activity can contribute to one's sense of isolation and unwantedness.[50] Martin Marty describes how people with chronic illnesses perceive others' attitudes and actions: "You aren't exactly a cheery person with whom people will want to keep company. You would brighten the scene by staying hidden. Take a pill to get out of your misery. Brighten up before you reappear. We have our own loads to carry. What makes you so special?"[51] While many people with chronic illnesses are often angry at the way people treat them, they often hesitate to express anger for fear of being isolated more or even abandoned.

Self-management of the illness becomes absolutely crucial, not only for a better quality of life, but also as a way to take responsibility for—even control of—one's own sense of well-being. There will always be decisions to make that involve risk, whether it has to do with taking medications that have side effects or going on an outing to the beach knowing that there is a good chance a setback will result because of it. But self-management of the illness is the primary way people not only survive but live well in the midst of the disease.[52]

Being in ministry with persons who live with chronic illnesses requires knowledge of the particular diseases and sensitivity to the many factors involved. Kerson describes some basic responses to avoid:

> Pretending that the illness does not exist is not helpful. Lending false hope that everything will be all right places extra stress on the individual to act well. This can be physically damaging to the person and damage your relationship. It is also important not to be so overly protective and do so much for the person that she feels devalued because she is unable to reciprocate.[53]

The woman described in Mark 5:25-34 has been living with her illness for twelve years. Her motivation for seeking healing is probably twofold: she wishes to be cleansed from her state of impurity and therefore be reintegrated into the community; and she wishes to be cured of a debilitating chronic illness. Seeking a cure out of sheer desperation is also a common response of those living with chronic illness today.

The Text
**Mark 5:25-34**

> [25]Now there was a woman who had been suffering from hemorrhages for twelve years. [26]She had endured much under many physicians, and had spent all that she had; and she was no better, but rather grew worse. [27]She had heard about Jesus, and came up behind him in the crowd and touched his cloak, [28]for she said, "If I but touch his clothes, I will be made well." [29]Immediately her hemorrhage stopped; and she felt in her body that she was healed of her disease. [30]Immediately aware that power had gone forth from him, Jesus turned about in the crowd and said, "Who touched my clothes?" [31]And his disciples said to him, "You see the crowd pressing in on you; how can you say, 'Who touched me?'" [32]He looked all around to see who had done it. [33]But the woman, knowing what had happened to her, came in fear and trembling, fell down before him, and told him the whole truth. [34]He said to her, "Daughter, your faith has made you well; go in peace, and be healed of your disease."

# Hermeneutics

This story of the woman who had a chronic illness for twelve years is often known as the story of the "hemorrhaging woman" or the "woman with the flow of blood." An abnormal menstrual flow is probably the cause of her situation.[54] Such a condition would render her "unclean" according to the Leviticus purity laws for as long as the condition continued and for another seven days after the flow of blood stopped (Lev. 15:25-30).

Not only would the woman be unclean, but anything she touched would also be unclean. Her husband and children, the bed she slept on, the clothes she wore, and the pots and plates she ate off of would all be polluted by her condition. Sexual relations were forbidden; after twelve years of living with this condition, she probably would have been totally alone and isolated from any social contact. Even if her condition had not been considered "unclean" by the purity laws, having a chronic illness for twelve years would have put a tremendous strain on her family situation. Weakness and fatigue alone would have curtailed her domestic responsibilities. Even without the purity laws, she may have been abandoned by family and friends.

According to Mark, the woman had spent money on physicians, so we know that at one time she had been a woman of some means. However, her fervent search for relief has left her in a state of poverty (common for many with chronic illnesses), impurity, and shame. She not only is religiously impure, but as a woman, she has also broken the social rules dictating gender roles in public life by appearing in public unaccompanied by a man. She is doubly outcast.

Mark includes this narrative in the middle of another story about a respected synagogue leader named Jairus, whose daughter is near death. Mark juxtaposes the two stories in order to point out unexpected reversals. Jairus is a respected synagogue leader of wealth, high on the social scale, who makes an appropriate request of Jesus by kneeling in deference to his authority (v. 22). He is pleading for his daughter, who is twelve years old and near death. In direct contrast to Jairus is this anonymous woman who is despised by all because of her impure state and lack of family or social relationships. She interrupts the vital missions of both Jesus and the important synagogue official. She approaches Jesus secretly and with cunning since she should not be in a public crowd—let alone touch anyone. She is pleading for herself since she has been sick and outcast for twelve years and is socially "dead." By the end of the narrative, however, the woman is cured and called "daughter."

*Verse 25:* Mark informs us from the beginning that a woman has been suffering for twelve years with an abnormal flow of blood. Whatever the cause, this condition has resulted in her being pronounced "unclean" and therefore being ostracized by the community, including her family. It has also meant twelve years without Temple worship or religious support. Though she is anonymous in this text, her story is repeated in the Acts of Pilate, chapter 7, in which she is remembered as Berenice.[55]

*Verse 26:* Whatever financial resources the woman once had have all been spent as she has sought help from various physicians. Instead of getting better, however, she has gotten worse. Poverty has been added to isolation and alienation.

*Verses 27-28:* The woman has heard about Jesus, comes up behind him in the crowd, and touches his cloak. This one verse (v. 27) says a great deal. Either out of sheer desperation or because she believes what she has heard about Jesus, the woman is willing to take an enormous risk just to be in a crowd, let alone to attempt to touch someone. As a woman, she would not be allowed to touch a strange man without his consent;[56] and as an "unclean" woman, she would be forbidden to touch any other person.

Touching Jesus' cloak as opposed to his person makes no difference, because touching the cloak would make it impure, and the person wearing the cloak would likewise become impure. The woman's act of touching Jesus' cloak implies that she believes Jesus to have divine powers, not simply healing powers. She believes she can be healed without Jesus' words or actions; her own faith along with touching his cloak will be sufficient.

The truth is, however, that she does not have much choice in how she approaches Jesus. To go to Jesus in the conventional way would mean having some man to accompany her and plead her case. The "patriarchal system precluded women from assertiveness in public life, interpersonally and socially."[57] There is no one left in her life, let alone a man to speak on her behalf. If she were to shout "unclean, unclean" as she is supposed to do in public, the crowd would never let her get close to Jesus. What she does breaks every convention relating to women and those considered "unclean." She is bold and assertive, secretive about her condition, and cunning. She formulates a plan to subvert the system, and she has the guts to carry it out. She has nothing to lose. She is already an outcast; what more can they do to her? She is already treated as if she were nonexistent, as if she were dead.

*Verse 29:* Immediately she knows that her flow of blood has stopped, and she instinctively feels it is more than just a temporary relief. Jesus does not say anything, he does not do anything. The healing happens purely by the woman's initiative and actions as she touches Jesus' cloak.

*Verses 30-31:* Jesus announces his own self-definition as one with miraculous knowledge and power as he turns in the crowd and asks, "Who touched me?"; and the disciples once more do not understand who Jesus is. They respond incredulously and in utter frustration: "You see the crowd pressing in on you; how can you say 'Who touched me?'" Why stop and ask such a ridiculous question when they are in a hurry to get to Jairus's house to heal the synagogue leader's daughter?

*Verses 32-33:* But Jesus pays no attention to the disciples' misapprehension, and he is in no hurry. He scans the crowd, but before he can identify who has touched him, the woman comes forward in "fear and trembling." Here is a bold, assertive, cunning woman who has broken all the rules to touch Jesus, and now she is tentative and filled with fear and trembling. What has happened? Mary Ann Tolbert offers one explanation:

> Her earlier "shameful" boldness in approaching Jesus was acceptable from one who was already banished from honorable society; but with her healing she may be reinstated in the religious and social community. Consequently, her timorous deference reflects her renewed conventional status as a woman in the male world of honor and shame.[58]

When the woman reaches Jesus, she falls at his feet and tells him the whole truth. Whether she falls at his feet because she expects to be scolded and judged because of her inappropriate behavior, or because she now fully believes Jesus to be divine, or both, we do not know. By telling Jesus the whole truth, she both confesses her actions and witnesses to Jesus' power. Her witness as a woman, however, would be highly suspect, if not unbelievable.

*Verse 34:* Jesus does not scold the woman for breaking the religious laws or for her outrageous behavior. Instead, he offers her something she has not had for twelve years—a relationship with another human being—when he addresses her as "daughter." Jesus says, "Daughter, your faith has made you well; go in peace, and be healed of your disease." In saying "your faith has made you well," Jesus is not making a healing statement—the cure has already taken place. Jesus is giving the woman credit for the healing rather than claiming the credit for himself. Both "faith" and "made you well" *(sozo)* were common terms associated with healing in non-Christian and non-Jewish Greek texts before and during the first century.[59] The mixed crowd would have understood what had taken place and what Jesus' actions meant in that context.

"Go in peace" was a standard Jewish blessing, whereas "be healed of your disease" comes from a Hellenistic blessing that means "take care of yourself so that you remain healthy," or "be healthy from your affliction."[60] "Jesus has combined a Jewish and Hellenistic blessing at the end of the story, creating a congenial social-rhetorical environment for a person who comes to Jesus from Jewish, Hellenic, or Jewish-Hellenic heritage."[61] Again, Jesus is speaking to the mixed crowd in language they all can understand. In this one sentence, Jesus is modeling for us the possibilities of inter-religious dialogue and multicultural communication.

We know nothing more of the woman, since her story is interrupted by a messenger from Jairus's house. The purity laws in Leviticus, however, would have required the bleeding to stop for at least seven days before she could perform the purification ritual and be pronounced "clean."

## Traditional Homiletic

The faith of the woman is often the focus of sermons on this text: her faith that the power of Jesus would be evident even through his clothing; or that "genuine faith means recognition, trust, and risk."[62] Some preach this text as one of the few examples of a *woman* of faith.

Another common theme denounces the foolishness of the woman who went to Jesus only as a last resort and the foolishness of the people today who also "spend their time seeking many physicians when all we need is Jesus."[63] This interpretation disregards the fact that Jesus was not around (he was barely out of his teens twelve years before) when the woman was seeking medical help. Furthermore, persons living with a chronic illness know that Jesus alone is not enough. I do not deny that faith is important in managing one's disease, but seeking medical help does not demonstrate a lack of faith. There are already too many horror stories of people who have followed their preachers' encouragement to rely on faith alone, who have stopped taking their medication or decided not to seek medical help, and who have died as a result.

From a feminist perspective, the woman's bold, assertive actions and her willingness to break the rules of society is lifted up. She is outrageously unconventional in her efforts to find wholeness for herself and her family. She blatantly disregards the social and religious norms that have kept her outcast, poor, and considered a nonentity within the community. She does not wait for anyone's permission, but rather takes the initiative for her own healing. Cure is not absolutely necessary, because women live with all kinds of minor and major diseases, but isolation from relationships with others is unbearable. All those who are outcast and rejected by society should likewise be bold and outrageous in acting on their own behalf and for the well-being of their communities, for Jesus still lifts up a model for a different kind of community—one in which the destitute and outcast are called "daughter."

## A Healing Homiletic

From the perspective of those who have a disability or a chronic illness, we see that the woman's actions may be motivated by sheer desperation rather than by faith. After twelve years of constantly washing soiled clothes in the midst of weakness, poverty, loss of family, and utter alienation from any human contact and support, sheer desperation may have been all the woman had left to impel her. Ostracized from the Temple and rejected because of the ritual purity laws, her faith in God and in traditional religion had probably waned after all these years. But Jesus is unconventional in his own way and provides a new vision of human community that would be very appealing to her.

The most shocking thing for the people in the crowd, however, would be that Jesus even has a conversation with a woman who is unaccompanied in public, who is "unclean," and who has clearly broken every rule in the book. By so doing, Jesus turns upside down not only the accepted concepts of honor and status, but also what is deemed appropriate and inappropriate, acceptable and unacceptable behavior. Without those rules for social interaction, life would seem chaotic.

Our society has certainly experienced this feeling of chaos in the past thirty years. Rules of social interaction—between men and women, between people of different cultures, between people with different sexual orientations—have all been challenged. A new vision of human community is before us, and for many, when the old rules of social interaction are set aside, life feels chaotic. But Jesus does not abide by the conventional rules. He affirms the woman's outrageous actions and sends her home in peace.

Jesus' use of language in the blessings of verse 34 communicates to both the Jewish community and the Hellenistic community. This provides a model for us today, as we learn to communicate across cultures and languages in ways that engender peace rather than alienation and hatred.

# CHAPTER SEVEN
# Mental Illness

There are only six narratives in the Gospels that deal with people who have a demon or an unclean spirit within them: (1) a "demoniac" who was mute (Matt. 9:32-34); (2) a "demoniac" who was blind and mute (Matt. 12:22-32; Luke 11:14-23; Mark 3:19b-30); (3) the daughter of the Syrophoenician or Canaanite woman (Mark 7:24-30, Matt. 15:21-28); (4) the man in the synagogue with the spirit of an unclean demon (Mark 1:21-28, Luke 4:31-37); (5) the boy with convulsions (Luke 9:37-43a, Mark 9:14-29, Matt. 17:14-21); and (6) the man from Gerasa who lived in the tombs (Luke 8:26-39, Mark 5:1-20, Matt. 8:28-34).

The Gospel of Mark uses the term "demon" or "demoniac" only in reference to the daughter of the Syrophoenician woman and the man from Gerasa who lived in the tombs. In all the other references, Mark uses the phrase "unclean spirit." The Gospel of John does not include any stories about Jesus casting out demons; all the texts in John that mention demons have to do with people accusing Jesus of having a demon (John 7:20; 8:48-52; 10:19-21). Jesus' actions and behavior seemed so bizarre to some that they said "He is possessed by a demon" (John 10:20).

There is so little information about the first four narratives listed above that it is difficult to comment on the nature of the "unclean spirit" or "demon." Since the boy with convulsions is included in the lectionary only as an optional addition to the Transfiguration text, it is not included here. I will discuss only Luke's account of the man from Gerasa.

159

Today, we would probably recognize this man's behavior as the result of some form of mental illness.

## Demon Possession in Biblical Times

Belief in demon possession was common in New Testament times, but this belief took various forms. What we find in the Gospels regarding demons is different from what we find in Paul's Epistles, and the Greek notion of demons differed from that of Palestinian Judaism. In the demonology of Greece, "Demons were considered to be the spirits of the dead or ghosts."[1] Demon possession could be beneficial as well as harmful. Good spirits could possess priestesses and inspire them to predict the future and to mediate between the gods and humanity. We find similar beliefs in other religions today in which benevolent gods and goddesses possess mediums or intermediaries in order to convey blessings or warnings to the faithful.

In the Gospels, however, demons are always malevolent, and angels are always benevolent. The demons or "unclean" spirits do only evil things, harming those they possess, while the "holy" spirit produces good results. In the Jewish context, the primary way to prevent demonic possession was to study the Torah and obey God's laws.[2] In the Christian context, manifesting the gifts of the Holy Spirit kept the demons away. Today, in some Christian contexts, the gift of speaking in tongues is the measure of whether one is "possessed" by the "holy" spirit or not.

Paul, however, was struggling against magicians who were casting out demons by magic. He believed demons to be evil forces and influences that could destroy people and keep them from believing in Jesus, but he condemned as sin any attempt to control them.[3] In the Synoptic accounts, surprisingly few of the many illnesses Jesus cured are attributed to demons. The references appear limited, and the symptoms of the illnesses were not readily explainable under the disease categories of Jesus' day.[4]

The Gospel writers included these texts to show Jesus' power over evil. Persons with unusual behavior become battlefields between good and evil rather than the main characters in the drama.[5] These narratives tell of an evil that has run rampant, taking control of people's lives without their consent, threatening destruction. When Jesus casts out the demon, he proclaims the "overthrow of arbitrary, violent and total oppression."[6]

The term "demon" is sometimes used as a metaphor today. Those who have an alcohol or drug addiction, those with certain kinds of mental illness, and those who feel their lives to be out of control may describe the experience as having a "demon" within. The metaphor deals with the feeling that something else has taken over one's life and will. But this is metaphorical usage and is not meant literally. It does not indicate a belief that an evil spirit has actually taken up habitation in the body.

What defines demon possession today is too complicated to discuss in this chapter. What is of concern however, is how we preach the texts that deal with demon possession. When a person has a form of epilepsy that cannot be totally controlled with medication or when someone has a mental illness, and we preach these texts by implying that such people are also possessed by demons, we add a tremendous burden to their already difficult lives. A mother writes of her son who struggled with epilepsy all his life:

> During various seizures, he almost drowned, he walked barefoot through a campfire, he was hit by a car, and laid in a snowbank nearly freezing to death. He went through his school years sitting in the hallway in a beanbag outside of the classroom so he would not be disruptive to the other students

when he had a seizure. In his early twenties he came to the realization that he was not possessed of a demon, but of a wonderfully courageous and valiant spirit![7]

What damage do we do to people's faith when we implicitly or explicitly proclaim that they are possessed by a demon? How do people deal with that label? What barriers do we erect between them and God? When they need the love and support of God, we tell them they are in league with the devil and imply that it is their fault. The messages do not have to be blatant. The subtle implications are sufficient to destroy what "courageous and valiant spirit" the person might have. When demon possession is equated with evil and epilepsy and mental illness are identified as demon possession in the Synoptics, then the message is conveyed that mental illness and epilepsy are evil.

No matter what one believes about demon possession, the lectionary text about the man from Gerasa who is mentally ill and the optional text about the boy with epilepsy should not be preached so as to imply that persons with epilepsy or mental illness today are possessed by demons. Persons who experience these illnesses, as well as their families and loved ones, suffer enough from social stigmas without the additional undue burden of being told they are possessed by demons.

## Mental Illness

The lectionary text that deals with demon possession is Luke's story of the man from Gerasa who lived in the tombs (Luke 8:26-39). The man's unexplained abnormal behavior leads many to believe he had a form of mental illness.[8]

Although the fields of medicine, psychiatry, and psychology have done much to inform us about the nature of various

162

forms of mental illnesses, there is still much to learn. The study of mental illnesses or mental disorders is very complex. For some mental disorders, the etiology or "patho-physiologic processes" are known, but for many, the etiology is unknown. Some may be rooted in biochemical imbalances while others probably stem from emotional or social causes. Most are the result of a combination of psychological, social, and biological factors. Abnormalities in brain structure and chemistry, genetics, environment, abuse, and family dynamics can all contribute to what are classified as various forms of mental illness.[9]

Mental illnesses cover a broad spectrum of disorders ranging from mild depression to schizophrenia. Mood and anxiety disorders, dissociative and delusional disorders, sleep and sexual disorders, and personality disorders are all classification categories for mental illnesses. Certain forms of mental illness may cause an individual to hear voices that instruct the individual what to say or do. Though this particular symptom may appear to many within the church to be some kind of spirit possession demanding an exorcism, an appropriate medical and psychiatric diagnosis by professionals is absolutely necessary to help the person begin the process of healing. When medication is necessary, a healing service that casts out the presumed "demon" may encourage the person not to take medication, and thus cause more harm than good.

Because of the many complexities involved in mental disorders, the classical distinction between neuroses and psychoses is no longer sufficient. Illnesses that are physiologically based in some form of biochemical imbalance are essentially no different from other biochemically induced illnesses, such as diabetes.[10] For those illnesses that are environmentally or characterologically based, the feelings and symptoms are very real and are beyond the individual's immediate control. In all cases, the process of healing is often long and arduous. Although medication and counseling help many people to manage the illness, instant cures are extremely rare. For many, living with a mental illness is a constant daily struggle, not only for the person with the illness, but also for the person's significant others. Mental illnesses are often chronic, depleting the energy, patience, and financial resources of the person and his or her family.

Persons with mental illness often feel they cannot trust their own thought processes and feelings. Like persons with physical disabilities, they have a sense of being betrayed by their own bodies. Persons who have physical disabilities often depend on their minds when their bodies are malfunctioning. It creates a mind/body dualism but can be a good coping strategy. For persons with mental illnesses, however, not being able to depend on their minds can feel like being betrayed by their own selves. This can greatly affect their self-image.

Unfortunately, mental illnesses have been accompanied by a tremendous social stigma that has differentiated mental illnesses from other forms of physical diseases and disabilities. In the religious sphere, some believe that what makes human beings in the image of God is our ability to reason. Severe mental illnesses often complicate an individual's reasoning ability; rationality can be impaired. Unfortunately, equating rationality with being human and being made in the image of God contributes to the oppression that many persons with mental illness experience. Church and society treat them as second-class citizens, often as less than human, and not fit for the sphere of the holy. Consciously or unconsciously, we label persons with mental illness "unclean" under our unspoken contemporary purity codes.

In the past, many people with mental illness who were considered unfit for society were put away in hospitals or institutions. However, in the 1980s many of the persons in mental institutions in this country were deinstitutionalized.

Persons with mental illness were sent back into society, where they could be a part of a local community and live in the mainstream of life rather than be isolated, out of the sight and consciousness of the rest of the world. Most communities and many local churches protested against deinstitutionalization and fought any attempt for group homes to be established in their surrounding areas. The result for persons with mental illness was not only further isolation and alienation, but also homelessness. Today, many of those who are homeless also have some form of mental illness.[11] It is impossible to be in ministry with the homeless population without also taking into consideration the issue of mental illness and its consequences in the lives of individuals.

The Text
**Luke 8:26-39**

26Then they arrived at the country of the Gerasenes, which is opposite Galilee. 27As he stepped out on land, a man of the city who had demons met him. For a long time he had worn no clothes, and he did not live in a house but in the tombs. 28When he saw Jesus, he fell down before him and shouted at the top of his voice, "What have you to do with me, Jesus, Son of the Most High God? I beg you, do not torment me"—29for Jesus had commanded the unclean spirit to come out of the man. (For many times it had seized him; he was kept under guard and bound with chains and shackles, but he would break the bonds and be driven by the demon into the wilds.) [30]Jesus then asked him, "What is your name?" He said, "Legion"; for many demons had entered him. [31]They begged him not to order them to go back into the abyss.

[32]Now there on the hillside a large herd of swine was feeding; and the demons begged Jesus to let them enter these. So he gave them permission. [33]Then the demons came out of the man and entered the swine, and the herd rushed down the steep bank into the lake and was drowned.

[34]When the swineherds saw what had happened, they ran off and told it in the city and in the country. [35]Then people came out to see what had happened, and when they came to Jesus, they found the man from whom the demons had gone sitting at the feet of Jesus, clothed and in his right mind. And they were afraid. [36]Those who had seen it told them how the one who had been possessed by demons had been healed. [37]Then all the people of the surrounding country of the Gerasenes asked Jesus to leave them; for they were seized with great fear. So he got into the boat and returned. [38]The man from whom the demons had gone begged that he might be with him; but Jesus sent him away, saying, [39]"Return to your home, and declare how much God has done for you." So he went away, proclaiming throughout the city how much Jesus had done for him.

## Hermeneutics

It is difficult to read this text and not sympathize with the homeless man living among the tombs, tortured by memories or by some illness he cannot control. Animal rights activists also scream out for mercy in regard to the herd of swine who seem to drown unnecessarily. Amidst all the pain and agony, however, is a carefully crafted text, rich with imagery and action.

Luke borrows both from oral tradition and from Mark's version of the story to include elements of surprise, unexpected twists, and foreshadowing.[12] Luke's straightforward narrative and complex symbolism provide interpreters a wealth of data to mine.

From the description of the tombs and the presence of pigs, the early Christians would have known that the story took place in Gentile territory. The tombs were considered unclean, and certainly swine were considered unclean animals. The country of the Gerasenes was a perfect place to house unclean spirits, since Gentile territory was already considered unclean according to Jewish law.[13] Yet once again Jesus is in the midst of the "unclean," challenging the purity codes. This story of a Gentile man who becomes a disciple of Jesus and a preacher and missionary to his own people, lays the groundwork for the evangelization of the Gentiles in Acts.[14]

The water imagery is also important. It was commonly believed that demons had an aversion to water (see Luke 11:24: "it wanders through waterless regions"). The water of baptism was used in early exorcisms, and even in this century, in colonial New England, accused "witches" were drowned (and the Wicked Witch of the West melts when touched by water in the *Wizard of Oz*).[15] Luke also places this text right after the scene in which Jesus shows his power over water by calming the sea and his disciples' fears in the midst of the storm. Here among the tombs, we encounter another terror and other fears.

The water imagery also conjures up images of the Exodus. As the oppressive legion of the Egyptian army was drowned in the sea, a legion of oppressive demons is drowned in the sea. Some scholars believe the military and political imagery of the word "Legion" and several other words is not by accident. "Herd" was also used for "military recruits or trainees"; Jesus' "dismissal" of the man in verse 38 "connotes a military command"; and "pigs charging" is reminiscent of "troops rushing into battle." The "demon" then, becomes the Roman military power, and the drowning of the demons signifies "political liberation from the might of Rome."[16] When a foreign country comes in and takes over, the foreign power is often seen not only as the enemy but metaphorically as the demon. The colonized country then, becomes "possessed by the demon."[17]

Other scholars take a socio-psychological approach to the text and make a connection between mental illness and political oppression: "It may well be that the word [Legion] haunted him because he had seen atrocities carried out by a Roman legion when he was a child . . . which left a scar upon his mind and ultimately sent him mad," writes William Barclay.[18] Ched Myers suggests that in the presence of economic exploitation and political repression, mental illness may be a "form of oblique protest against, or escape from, oppression." He continues: "The 'colonization of the mind' in which the community's anguish over its subjugation is repressed and then turned in on itself, is perhaps implied by Mark's report that the man inflicts violence on himself."[19]

This narrative may be one that tells the story of a community that is politically and economically oppressed, a community that feels it is controlled by demonic foreign powers over which it has no control. But it is also the story of a man who used to live in the city, but who has become so tortured within that he has been cast out of the community, and is now homeless, naked, living among the tombs, and no longer in control of his own identity and actions. Unlike Mark, Luke makes a very clear distinction between the man who is tormented and the "demons."[20] Jesus relates to the man as well as to the "demons" and sends the man back home again.

*Verse 26:* The exact name of the city nearby where Luke says Jesus disembarks is ambiguous at best. "Gadarenes" and "Gerasenes" are used by different authors. Luke's version uses "Gerasenes." However, the city of Gerasa is thirty miles from the sea[21] and none of the other names match that of a city close to the waterfront. Luke's description is vague enough: "They arrived at the country of the Gerasenes, which is opposite Galilee." The exact location is not important to the text. It is near the sea in Gentile territory.

*Verse 27:* Several bits of information are provided here about the man. He was originally from a city, but now he has demons. For a long time he has not worn clothes nor has he lived in a house. The text implies that he had once had a relatively normal life, living in a home in the city. Yet once he began having problems, he was forced out of his home and out of the city. His life became unmanageable and his behavior was sometimes uncontrollable. Alienated from family and friends, he now lives alone in the tombs. It could have been possible to actually live in the tombs, since many were carved-out caves in the rocks of the mountains. Tombs were not only considered unclean places for the Jews, they were also considered the dwelling place of demons in popular thought. Living among the dead, he lived as if dead to the rest of his community.

It is not uncommon today to find persons with various mental illnesses alienated from their families and friends. As normal, everyday activities become more unmanageable and behavior becomes erratic and even uncontrollable, many persons find themselves cast out of their homes. Some are relegated to mental institutions, and others end up in the hewn-out doorways of cement buildings, the tombs of the streets.

*Verse 28:* According to Luke, when the man sees Jesus, he falls down before him and shouts, "What have you to do with me, Jesus, Son of the Most High God? I beg you, do not torment me." The term "Son of the Most High God" is a Hellenistic title rather than a Jewish title and therefore would be appropriate in Gentile territory.[22] More so in Mark's Gospel, but also in Luke, the disciples do not totally understand who Jesus is. Here, Luke presents a Gentile who understands exactly who Jesus is: Son of the Most High God.

The term translated "torment" can also mean "torture" or "testing." Luke has the reader believe that it is the demon talking rather than the man himself.

Today, persons with dissociative personality disorders (multiple personalities), those who hear voices, even those who are addicted to substances, often feel that someone or something else is in control of their thoughts, their words, and their actions. These experiences can both torment and torture persons as they struggle with what is happening and why.

*Verse 29:* Luke backtracks and explains why the man or "demon" responds in this way. The demon evidently is not always in total control of the man's life but has "seized him" many times. In the past the man has been kept under guard and bound with chains and shackles because of his behavior, but he has broken the bonds and been driven out into the wilds.

The chains and shackles are reminiscent of straitjackets and other restraints that are used today for persons with mental illness whose behavior is dangerous to themselves or to others. It is an external form of control. With proper medication and therapy, some are able to break through the chains and shackles to return to society. Others break through the chains only to be driven out into a hostile world to wander in the wilds.

*Verse 30:* Jesus asks the man his name, and the reply is "Legion." "Legion" simply means "a multitude," or "many," and at the time of Jesus the term was used almost solely in military contexts. The term "conjures up the vision of an army of occupation, cruelty, and destruction."[23] Henceforth Luke drops the singular form of address, and uses the plural. Naming was a powerful thing during the time of Jesus. Knowing in whose name one's power came was important, which is why early Christians performed exorcisms "in the name of Jesus." But it was also important to have power over the name of the one who was to be exorcised, which is why Jesus asks its name. Jesus is trying to make contact with the man behind the demon.

Making contact with people who live with severe mental illnesses is very important and not always easy. Family and friends feel a sense of loss—that the person they used to know is "not there" anymore, or at least not the same. For some people, the mental disorder does take over not only their lives, but also their identities. Making a connection with the person in the midst of the disorder can bring a healing touch.

*Verse 31:* The abyss is a term that refers to the demons' place of origin,[24] the "depths or pit to which the dead or evil spirits are consigned."[25]

*Verse 32:* Not wanting to go into the abyss, Legion begs Jesus to let them enter the swine. In Gentile territory it was not uncommon to see many pigs, but swine do not travel in herds, so many swineherds were required. Consequently, the

swineherds and pigs would have been all over the countryside. From time to time, many probably would have come in
contact with the man living in the tombs.

*Verse 33:* The demons enter the swine and the swine rush
off the cliff into the sea and drown. Although some people
question Jesus' right to take away the livelihood of the
swineherds and others question the necessity of killing innocent pigs, it was important to Luke's original audience to
hear that the demons not only leave the man, but also are
totally destroyed. For the demons to go wandering around
in space would not be acceptable, for it was believed that
demons preferred to inhabit something.[26] Simply transfer-
ring their habitation from the man to the pigs would not be
sufficient, because the swine would still be in the area, and
the people believed the demons in the pigs could then ran-
domly decide to take control of someone else's life. By
reporting that the pigs drown in the water, Luke put the
concerns of the people to rest, since water was understood
as a sure form of destruction for demons.

Since pigs do not move in herds, and since they are more
likely to panic and scatter than to move in a group, "the
miracle in the story lay in the pigs' forming themselves up to
two thousand strong, and rushing over the cliff."[27] This
untypical behavior would be viewed by the swineherds as a
supernatural event—as evidence that the pigs are spooked
or bewitched or possessed. This is the swineherds' proof that
the demons are now in the swine.[28] The unusual action of
the pigs also gives visible evidence to the man that his
demons are truly gone and will not "seize him" at another
time.

If only ridding oneself of mental illness were that easy!
Setting animal rights aside, it would be worth the cost of a
pig farm to have the assurance that one would not be tormented or "seized" by mental illness again. But the truth is
that managing mental illness can be a very slow and arduous

process. It is longer and much harder to do alone. The healing process is quickened when strong support systems are present: friends and family who have the time and energy that is often required, health insurance, trained doctors and therapists, and a strong faith. Simply casting out the so-called "demon" in the name of Jesus is not always sufficient. Medication is often crucial. And yet an accepting and supportive faith community is very important in the healing process.

*Verse 34:* The swineherds flee when they see what has happened and run to tell the townsfolk. They are amazed and shocked at the events, but they also might want to make sure they are not blamed for the destruction of the pigs. They certainly are not in a rejoicing mood. Theirs is not a leave-taking filled with excitement and thanksgiving for what Jesus has done for the man.

*Verse 35:* The townspeople come out to see for themselves what the swineherds are talking about. When they arrive, they find the man sitting at the feet of Jesus, clothed and in his right mind. "Sitting at the feet of Jesus" is a phrase used to denote discipleship; it is applied to those who are learning the teachings of Jesus to become one of his followers. The man's sense of reality and appropriate social behaviors have returned, and he has put on clothes. We are also told "he is in his right mind." The Greek term *sophronounta* denotes "sobriety and clear sightedness."[29]

But the townspeople are afraid. Instead of responding with awe and wonder, celebrating the positive change in the man's life, the townspeople are frightened. They are afraid of what they do not understand.

Today, fear is often the cause of people avoiding persons with mental illness. The fear is often unfounded—a result of not understanding what seems "abnormal" behavior or speech. People feel afraid when they see a homeless man wandering down the street talking to himself, or a woman walking in circles, swatting at an unseen object. This fear is not based on factual knowledge that the person is dangerous; it is aroused simply by the unknown and, for some, the unknowable.

*Verse 36:* "Those who had seen it," tell the townspeople how the man has been "healed." Here Luke uses the Greek term *sozo*, which was used often by Mark and can also mean "saved."

*Verse 37:* According to Luke, all the people ask Jesus to leave because they are "seized with great fear." It had been the demon, which often "seized" the man, that had caused him to do irrational things. Now, it is the demon called "fear" that seizes all the people and causes them to do what seems to be an irrational act—to send Jesus away. There are no congratulations to the man—no conversation between the townsfolk and the man at all. Their fear has taken control of their lives, and out of ignorance, they ask Jesus to depart from them. It may be that their fear is based in superstition, but for whatever reason, this display of power is so far beyond their comprehension that they do not want to deal with its reality.

Luke jumps ahead of himself and informs us that Jesus does what the people ask: he gets into the boat and returns to the other shore. However, the story has not ended; there is one last conversation between the man and Jesus.

*Verse 38:* The man begs Jesus to allow him to stay with him, supposedly to follow him and be one of his disciples. Often those who are helped become dependent upon their helpers, whether the helpers be doctors, therapists, or ministers. It is more difficult to go back to the community that has developed opinions about who one is and what one is capable or not capable of doing than to stay in the surroundings of those who have assisted in the healing process, those who know how far one has come, those who accept and believe in the one who has struggled. But Jesus does not let the man stay or become physically dependent upon him. Instead, Jesus dismisses him and sends him home to get on with his new life.

*Verse 39:* The man has not lived in a home for a long time, but now Jesus says, "Return to your home, and declare how much God has done for you." Jesus not only sends him back into the community, but also entrusts him with a great responsibility. Jesus clearly gives credit to God and wants the Gentile to become a believer in the grace and love of God. The man does go and proclaim throughout the city, but instead of proclaiming what God had done for him, he proclaims what Jesus has done for him. In this twist of terms, Luke is proclaiming his belief that God is clearly at work in Jesus.

The Greek word *kerysso* is the "standard verb for apostolic preaching."[30] The man who has lived so long in the tombs becomes not only a follower of Jesus but a preacher as well. He is a missionary to his own people. Almost two thousand years ago, Jesus knew the importance of using people indigenous to an area for missionary work! Who else would be better able to communicate to the people in a way they could understand? Who else could break through their fear other than the one who had experienced the acceptance and grace offered by God through Jesus? On the other hand, was it not Jesus who said "Truly I tell you, no prophet is accepted in the prophet's hometown" (Luke 4:24)? Preaching to one's own people can be a very difficult task, but the man accepts the challenge and responsibility and sets forth on a new life.

## *Traditional Homiletic*

Because this text is so full of rich imagery and exciting events, it has been preached in many different ways over the centuries. Jesus' power over evil is certainly one of the Gospel writer's main themes for this text. There is a problem, however, in equating mental illness with evil. There are some forms of mental illness—such as post-traumatic stress disorder—that are caused by violent acts witnessed or experienced, and these violent acts can clearly be labeled evil. But there are other forms of mental illness that are caused by chemical imbalances within one's brain. These are the types of mental illness that cause some people to feel betrayed by their own bodies, their own minds, their own selves. Some persons living with mental illness are able to differentiate the illness from the self and choose to name the illness "evil" because of its effects. For many, however, the line between the illness and the self is thin or nonexistent, and to name the illness evil is often to name the person evil as well. We need to take care not to equate the person with evil.

Another common theme preached on this text is that of evangelism or the need for "missionary work that begins at home."[31] Some emphasize that even though the townsfolk do not want Jesus around and send him away, Jesus has the "last word" by sending one of their own to witness to them.[32] But in today's world, that sounds more like oppressive imperialism than the compassion and love Jesus intends.

Some preachers still focus on demons and the need for exorcisms, and some have related demonic possession to "bondage of sin."[33] But in the New Testament, demon possession is not related to a person's sin. Rather, it is understood to be an undeserved, vicious, random act of the evil spirits.

Others focus on the psychological aspects of the text. They deal with the human situation and stress that "curing and saving will involve suffering" or that it is easier to " 'escape' from our wretchedness than fully and honestly to recognize and seek to understand it."[34] Although both of these statements may be true for some people, for those with severe mental illness the first is not a strong message of hope and the second adds blame to the person who is already struggling.

The political oppression theme that some biblical scholars have raised could provide some interesting twists on this text. Any country or culture experiencing oppression from a foreign force can relate to the dynamics in this text. The history of African Americans in this country tells the story of a people controlled by a "legion" of foreigners who possessed them. The Korean community knows what it is like to have their homeland occupied by a foreign country. Their history witnesses to the cruel atrocities committed against Korean women in Japanese military comfort camps. The man in the text becomes a symbol for the larger community that is controlled by outside evil forces and the tremendous damage to the community's identity that results. Jesus then becomes the figure who destroys the evil powers as the pigs rush over the cliff into the sea and drown. This may be a message of hope for many who are oppressed, but it also raises questions of when violence and war are justified.

## A Healing Homiletic

What would be a healing touch, a message of hope for people who have some association with mental illness who are sitting in the pew? It is a very frightening thing to feel out of control of one's own thoughts, behavior, and even identity. Families worry about their loved ones who live with mental illnesses, but often their own personal, financial, and psychological resources have been so strained that they, too, need a respite from the illness. Adding more guilt to their lives is neither helpful nor a message of hope or healing.

A common element that runs throughout many of the healing narratives is Jesus' compassion to those who have reached the "limits of human desperation"[35]—those who are on the very edges of society—and how Jesus returns them to their homes, their relationships, and their rightful places within the community. Jesus reaches out to those who are alienated, to those who are homeless, to those who are in the depths of despair, and offers them respect and a sense of belonging.

God's intent for our lives is for us to be at "home," clothed, and in our right minds. Jesus breaks through the purity codes and social conventions that forbid him to be among the tombs and among the Gentiles. Jesus reaches out to the man who seems beyond hope. He enables the man to regain control of his own life, and then Jesus trusts him with responsibility as he sends him back home to preach the good news. Trusting the man with responsibility was a strong gesture of respect on Jesus' part. It gave purpose and a sense of meaning to the man's life. He was able to contribute something back into the community, to be an interdependent part of the whole rather than being totally dependent upon others. That is an important part of the healing process for those with severe mental illnesses. It should be taken slowly, but trusting them with responsibility and giving them meaning in life as an interdependent part of the community is very important.

It needs to be stressed, however, that although the man in the text is supposedly "cured" in an instant, this is not the experience of most persons with severe mental illnesses today. The text does teach us a very important lesson: Jesus does not let the man stay in his physical presence. He sends him out to be a missionary to his own people. Being a follower or disciple of Jesus means being the hands and feet and words of hope and healing for Jesus in our own place

and time. Caring for, communicating with, and understanding persons who suffer from feeling as if they are
controlled by outside forces is up to us as Jesus' present day
disciples. We can be a supportive and healing presence to
them on their journeys.

As ordained ministers and active laypersons, it may be
that we need to understand that it is often doctors and
psychiatrists who "stand in for" Jesus today, who understand
what is necessary for curing or managing the illness. But this
does not mean that the local church community should
delegate the entire healing process to those within the medical fields. There is much that a strong faith and a supportive,
healing community can offer to persons living with mental
illness and to their families. There is also much that persons
with mental illness can contribute to the various ministries
of the church. But for healing and full participation to
happen, the church and society must deal with their own
feelings of being "seized with fear" when in the presence of
something they do not understand. Fear is often the greatest
barrier to healing—both for those who need the healing and
for those who offer a helping hand. It is fear that causes the
townsfolk in the text to act irrationally and send Jesus away.
Jesus has control over the raging storm, the tempestuous sea,
and the "legion" that had taken control of the man's behavior,
but he cannot or does not control the fear that seizes the
townsfolk. We need to address our irrational fears before we
can be a healing presence in the lives of those who live with
mental illness.

# CHAPTER EIGHT

# A Healing Homiletic

You might be feeling a little overwhelmed at this point, seriously contemplating choosing the Epistle or Old Testament lesson of the day whenever one of these Gospel narratives appears in the lectionary. But do not dismay. Through our struggle with preaching these texts in a way that is healing and liberative for persons with disabilities, we can contribute to an attitude of welcoming acceptance of persons with disabilities both in our churches and in society.

So how can preachers prepare sermons on these texts that are faithful to the text and not oppressive to persons who live with disabilities today? What does it mean to preach the healing texts today in a way that is liberative and healing for those who have similar disabilities as those described in the Gospel narratives? Do I suggest that all sermons on these texts should be preached only to persons with disabilities? No. Do I suggest that preachers should seriously consider the lived reality and experiences of persons with those particular disabilities when preparing sermons on these texts? Absolutely yes. If we do not, the very people Jesus healed and welcomed into the family of God will be rejected and ostracized from the faith communities of today.

The realities of persons with disabilities today force pastors to analyze their own theologies about disability and suffering. Are persons with disabilities blessed or cursed, angels or demons? What is God's role in their lives? What do we say when they ask, "Why did this happen to me?" One's theology clearly influences how one preaches these texts. We must be clear about our own theologies so that we do not communicate something we do not believe.

Many literal interpretations of the text explicitly or implicitly communicate that disability is a result of someone's sin or lack of faith, when in reality, a careful examination of these texts shows that in many instances Jesus does not require faith before healing and in John 9 denies that sin is the cause of the disability. Metaphorical interpretations of these texts have the same effect, although the approach and theology are very different. Using sensory language such as *"deaf* to God's voice" or *"blind* to the will of God" equates the existential reality of persons with disabilities with lack of faith or a broken relationship with God—in other words, sin. Rather than encouraging one's faith in God—faith that is often crucial for the daily survival of those who live with a disability—literal and metaphorical interpretations of these texts erect stumbling blocks in the path of faith. The young man with epilepsy does not need to be told he has a demon. Instead he needs to be encouraged to recognize God's gift to him of a courageous and undauntable spirit.

There are millions of persons today who live with a wide variety of physical and mental disabilities. Many diseases and psychological disorders can be *cured*, but for most of the disabilities represented in these Gospel texts, *cure* is rare today. This does not mean, however, that *healing* is not possible in the lives of persons who live with these disabilities. We should keep in mind the difference between *cure* and *healing* so that we are not using the words interchangeably. Although *cure* almost always means healing, the opposite is not true; *healing* often does not mean *cure*. Healing happens in a wide variety of ways, in many aspects of a person's life. Healing can happen in the lives of persons who live with physical deafness, blindness, paralysis, Hansen's disease, and severe forms of mental illness, through various medical and technological means and through guidance on how to manage their particular disabilities well. Healing often occurs through the loving presence of another person.

I want to briefly discuss the reemergence of healing services in many mainline Protestant churches today, since these texts are often used when preaching is included in those services. Although healing services are very important for a wide variety of people, they can be oppressive for those who have permanent, incurable disabilities when the emphasis is on *cure* rather than *healing*. This is not to deny the power of prayer or the possibility of miracles, but too often a healing service (with an emphasis on cure) for persons who are blind or deaf or paralyzed implies that these persons are not acceptable *as they are*. It says that there is something wrong with them, often something "sinful" or "evil" about their condition or existence, and only physical "wholeness" is welcomed in the sphere of the holy. On the other hand, healing services that focus on the *healing* of broken relationships and the isolation some experience from the community and important people in their lives can be very important. Services that build people's self-esteem and inner strength to handle the problems they face can be truly *healing*.

An underlying question we can ask as we prepare to preach on these texts is, "What is healing for persons with disabilities today?" It is not only a homiletical question, but also a pastoral care issue and a theological quandary for some.

In many situations, it is not the physical aspect of a disability that needs healing the most. The statement, "If someone offered me a cure, I'd take it, but I don't need it," sums up what many people with permanent disabilities feel.

It would be nice not to have to live with the limitations posed by the physical disability, but it is the social isolation and alienation people experience that is the most difficult. Most people would rather get on with living—developing meaningful interdependent relationships in a caring community—rather than spend their limited energy and finances on seeking a cure. If our preaching is to facilitate reconciliation and healing of relationships rather than isolation from the gathered community, we must develop a new, healing homiletic. As a starting point, I offer five observations and suggestions.

1. In preaching these texts, comparisons can be made, as long as sensory language is not used, in relationship to sin. Instead of saying we are *blind, deaf, mute,* or *paralyzed* to the will of God, we should say what we mean: "we do not understand who Jesus is," "we ignore God's will for our lives," "we do not testify to God's presence in our world," "we refuse to act on God's behalf," and so on. I realize that homiletical literature stresses metaphorical language because of its richness. But in this case, at whose expense? We know now that using *black* and *white* metaphorically (so that *black* equals evil and *white* equals purity) contributes to negative attitudes toward people who are Black. Likewise, using sensory language such as *deaf* and *blind* in relationship to sin supports negative attitudes towards those who live with disabilities. It is best to avoid equating the physical reality of disability with these "sinful" behaviors of others.

2. Another way to preach these texts without using sensory language is to look at the situation of the person with the disability in the text. Most of the people with disabilities described in the texts are ostracized and rejected by their social and religious communities, not because of some sinful act they committed, but simply because of some aspect of who they are—some part of their being. In our pluralistic

and multicultural communities it is important to ask, "When have you been isolated or ostracized from your community because of who you are, not by what you have done?" or, "When have we isolated or ostracized someone from our community because of our own fears about who they are?"

3. But most shocking to the first-century audience of these narratives were the many cultural and religious boundaries Jesus crossed. In touching the man with leprosy, Jesus breaks the ritual purity code. Jesus should become ritually unclean himself; but instead, the man with leprosy is no longer outcast, and he returns to his family and religious community. In the story of the woman with the flow of blood, we are told that Jesus stops and recognizes the woman's touch. Here is a woman who is not supposed to be in public unaccompanied by a man—an unclean woman who is supposed to keep her distance and shout "Unclean" as she passes by. But Jesus stops, recognizes her, and calls her "daughter."

We might not have written purity codes today, but in our churches and our society, we certainly have unwritten purity codes—implicit understandings of who is acceptable and who is not. These boundaries are often drawn along economic and racial lines, or according to someone's idea of what is acceptable for the sphere of the holy and what is not. Those who are homeless, those whose behavior is affected by some form of mental illness, those whose physical appearance is considered unacceptable, those whose sexual orientation is different from the norm—all fall outside the boundaries drawn by our purity codes. What unwritten purity codes are operating in your congregation? What boundaries have our communities of faith established to protect themselves from those considered unclean today?

4. In preaching these texts, one could also emphasize the actions of the person with the disability in the text. On the

margins of society, expected to be passive and out of sight so they can also be out of society's mind, Bartimaeus, the woman with the flow of blood, the man with leprosy, and the Syrophoenician woman all take matters into their own hands. They are bold and active, taking the initiative in their own journey toward well-being. The crowd tries to silence Bartimaeus. Jesus tries to silence the Syrophoenician woman when he says, "It is not right to take the children's bread and throw it to the dogs." But in the end, their perseverance and boldness is rewarded by a deep healing. How can we enable people in their search for well-being when our tendency is to judge those who take the initiative—when we feel they should stay on the margins?

5. Another way to preach some of these texts is to focus on the response of the crowds. In the story of the boy with epilepsy, the crowd gathers around gawking. Some are curious as to why the disciples were ineffective in curing the boy, others stand in revulsion at the boy's bizarre behavior, while others have come to wonder at the power of Jesus. But in the story of the man who was living in the tombs, the one they called "Legion," the crowd is seized with fear at what Jesus has done, and they send Jesus away.

The crowd surrounding Bartimaeus tries to shut him up—they try to make him sit down and behave like a proper blind beggar. But it only takes the attention of one respected leader to change the crowd's attitude. When Jesus stops and calls Bartimaeus to him, the crowd changes its tune. How do we respond to the unfamiliar, the out-of-the-ordinary, those who are unlike us? Are we seized with fear? Do we try to make them "go away"? Or do we simply try to silence those who are different from us? Do we enforce an expectation of passivity—out of sight and out of mind—on those we consider less important than us? Or maybe we are just among the curious bystanders. Where are the leaders today who are willing to stop and model attention to and respect for those on the margins?

In prayer and study you will find many more possibilities for preaching these texts. I have presented a theology that denies the belief that God causes disabilities for whatever reason. I do not believe that my disability or anyone else's is the will of God. I do, however, strongly believe that God's presence infuses our lives with strength and grace and love to manage whatever struggles come our way. God wills the well-being of each one of us at every moment of our lives. At the same time, we are all interdependent upon one another and upon the natural world. God depends on us to be God's agents of healing in the world as much as we depend on God to undergird us with everlasting love and care.

I began this book with the story about the unfortunate death of a young man, Sig. There is another story, however.

A little girl was late getting home from school. Her mother became more and more worried as the afternoon wore on. When she finally arrived, the mother said, "Where have you been?! I've been worried sick!" The little girl responded, "Well, I was almost home, but then I saw Suzie sitting on the curb crying. Her dolly was broken." Her mother, relieved, said, "Oh! So you stopped to help her fix her dolly?" The little girl with the wisdom of the universe said, "No. I sat down on the curb, and I helped Suzie cry."[1]

Whenever we struggle in life, God sits beside us and helps us cry. May our preaching of these texts bring a healing presence into the lives of persons with disabilities and all those who struggle in our wounded world.

# Notes

## Introduction

1. There is a shift taking place in the nature of healing liturgies that began with impetus from the feminist community. A wide variety of healing rituals have been created for women undergoing divorce, miscarriage, breast cancer, and menopause. These types of healing rituals are slowly making their way into mainstream denominations.

## 1. Healing and Theodicy

1. See Nancy Eiesland, *The Disabled God* (Nashville: Abingdon, 1994). Eiesland deals with this issue at length. She says that "disability denotes an unusual relationship with God . . . either divinely blessed or damned" (p. 70).

2. David A. Pailin, *A Gentle Touch* (London: Society for Promoting Christian Knowledge, 1992), 71.

## 2. Hermeneutical Hazards

1. John J. Pilch, "Understanding Healing in the Social World of Early Christianity," *Biblical Theology Bulletin* 22, no. 1 (spring 1992): 27-30.

2. Ibid., 28.

3. John J. Pilch, "Healing in Mark: A Social Science Analysis," *Biblical Theology Bulletin* 11, no. 4 (Oct. 1981): 143.

4. Ibid.

5. Ibid.

6. John J. Pilch, "The Health Care System in Matthew: A Social Science Analysis," *Biblical Theology Bulletin* 16, no. 3 (July 1986): 102.

7. For more information about purity codes, see chapter 6.

8. John J. Pilch, "Sickness and Healing in Luke-Acts," in *The Social World of Luke-Acts*, ed. Jerome Neyrey (Peabody, Mass.: Hendrickson, 1991), 206.

9. Pilch, "Healing in Mark: A Social Science Analysis," 143, paraphrasing Arthur Kleinman, *Patients and Healers in the Context of Culture* (Berkeley: UCLA Press, 1980), 82.

10. Pilch, "Sickness and Healing in Luke-Acts," 207.

11. See Reginald H. Fuller, *Interpreting the Miracles* (Philadelphia: Westminster, 1963), 125.

12. Similar challenges are being brought by African Americans concerning the metaphorical usage of "black" and "white." "Black" is used metaphorically to denote a negative, evil, sinful element, while "white" denotes purity and goodness. The use of language is a symbolic act, and when words and symbols are always used in negative terms, the language contributes to the oppressive way people view and treat those who have blindness or blackness as part of their essential identity. Language does make a difference. The entire nongendered or inclusive language movement among feminist Christians is an attempt to make this point.

13. Halford E. Luccock, exposition to "The Gospel According to St. Mark," in *The Interpreter's Bible* (Nashville: Abingdon, 1951), 7:820.

14. Eduard Schweizer, *The Good News According to Mark* (Atlanta: John Knox, 1977), 58.

15. Luccock, exposition to "Mark," 757.

# 3. Blindness

1. See Raymond E. Brown, *The Anchor Bible: The Gospel According to John (i-xii)* (Garden City, N.Y.: Doubleday, 1966), 378.

2. Marian Soards, Thomas Dozeman, and Kendall McCabe, *Preaching the Revised Common Lectionary: Year A—Lent/Easter* (Nashville: Abingdon, 1992), 69.

3. Reginald H. Fuller, *Preaching the New Lectionary* (Collegeville, Minn.: Liturgical Press, 1971), 158.

4. See J. Louis Martyn, *History and Theology in the Fourth* Gospel, rev. ed. (Nashville: Abingdon, 1979), 24-36.

5. Brown, *John*, 379.

6. Soards, Dozeman, and McCabe, *Preaching the Revised Common Lectionary: Year A—Lent/Easter*, 70.

7. Arthur John Gossip, exposition to "The Gospel According to St. John," in *The Interpreter's Bible* (Nashville: Abingdon, 1952), 8:613.

8. Ibid., 612.

9. Robert M. Price, "Illness Theodicies in the New Testament," *Journal of Religion and Health* 25, no. 4 (winter 1986): 314.

10. Gossip, exposition to "John," 8:614.

11. Brown, *John*, 380.

12. Fuller, *Preaching the New Lectionary*, 159.

13. See Brown, *John*, 380.

14. Ibid., 375.

15. William Barclay, *The Gospel of John*, rev. ed. (Philadelphia: Westminster, 1975), 2:50.

16. F. B. Craddock et al., *Preaching the New Common Lectionary: Year A—Lent, Holy Week, Easter* (Nashville: Abingdon, 1986), 60.

17. Gossip, exposition to "John," 8:612.

18. Brown, *John*, 380.

19. Ibid., 381.

20. Paul Achtemeier, "And He Followed Him: Miracles and Discipleship in Mark 10:46-52," *Semeia* 11 (1978): 122.

21. Antoinette Clark Wire, "The Structure of the Gospel Miracle Stories and Their Tellers," *Semeia* 11 (1978): 84.

22. Ibid., 100.

23. Reginald H. Fuller, *Interpreting the Miracles* (Philadelphia: Westminster, 1963), 35.

24. Some scholars believe that the Bartimaeus event actually took place as Jesus and his disciples were passing through on their way to Jerusalem for the Feast of Tents rather than for Passover. See Fred Craddock and Leander Keck, *Proclamation: Pentecost 3—Series B* (Philadelphia: Fortress, 1976), 26.

25. Achtemeier, "And He Followed Him," 128.

26. Fuller, *Preaching the New Lectionary*.

27. Perry H. Biddle, *Preaching the Lectionary: A Workbook for Year B* (Louisville, Ky.: Westminster/John Knox, 1990), 313.

28. Halford E. Luccock, exposition to "The Gospel According to St. Mark," in *The Interpreter's Bible* (Nashville: Abingdon, 1951), 7:820.

29. Ched Myers, *Binding the Strong Man: A Political Reading of Mark's Story of Jesus* (Maryknoll, N.Y.: Orbis, 1988), 282.

30. Achtemeier, "And He Followed Him," 120.

31. Wire, "Structure," 101.

32. Craddock and Keck, *Proclamation: Pentecost 3—Series B*, 23.

33. Achtemeier, "And He Followed Him," 134.

34. Earl S. Johnson, "Mark 10:46-52: Blind Bartimaeus," *Catholic Biblical Quarterly* 40 (1978): 201.

35. K. C. Hanson, *Proclamation 4: Series B, Pentecost 3* (Minneapolis: Augsburg Fortress, 1991), 35.

36. Fuller, *Preaching the New Lectionary*, 441.

37. Craddock and Keck, *Proclamation: Pentecost 3— Series B*, 24.

38. Biddle, *Preaching the Lectionary: A Workbook for Year B*, 314.

39. Craddock and Keck, *Proclamation: Pentecost 3— Series B*, 24.

40. Myers, *Binding the Strong Man*, 282.

41. William Barclay, *The Gospel of Mark*, rev. ed. (Philadelphia: Westminster, 1975), 261.

42. Johnson, "Mark 10:46-52: Blind Bartimaeus," 201.

# 4. Deafness and Hearing Loss

1. In Mark's account of the boy with epilepsy, it is implied that an unclean spirit renders the boy unable to speak or hear. An unconscious state, however, is part of a tonic-clonic seizure, and therefore the boy would be unresponsive. This unresponsiveness does not mean that the boy was physically deaf or mute.

2. While it is true that most persons with disabilities prefer to be identified as persons first (for example, "a person who is paralyzed"), this is not often the case in the Deaf Culture. Those in the Deaf Culture perceive themselves not as persons with disabilities but rather as members of a linguistic and cultural minority group. They take pride in their culture, their language, and their deaf identity. The terms "the deaf" and "deaf person" are very common in the community and will be used in this chapter.

3. The deaf community is comprised of persons whose levels of hearing loss range from mild to profound and who communicate in a range of communication modes and signed and spoken languages. Within this broad group is a group of people who consider themselves to be part of what is called the *Deaf Culture*: they are usually deaf children born to deaf parents, their first language is usually American Sign Language, and they have been raised according to the worldview and values of the Deaf Culture. In order to distinguish this group from others who have an audiological hearing loss, the term "Deaf" with a capital "D" is used to refer to the members of the Deaf Culture, and the term "deaf" with a lower-case "d" is used to refer to members of the deaf community that encompasses a wider variety of languages, communication modes, and cultural orientations. For a more detailed discussion of Deaf Culture, deaf community, and the use of "Deaf" versus "deaf," see Carol Paddon and Tom Humphries, *Deaf in America: Voices from a Culture* (Cambridge, Mass.: Harvard University Press, 1988).

4. For the purposes of this chapter, I will use "English" as an example of a common spoken language. However, oralism can apply to any native spoken language—Spanish, Korean, Tongan, etc. Likewise, I will be using American Sign Language as the indigenous language of the Deaf Culture here in America, but each country has its own indigenous sign language as well.

5. Reginald H. Fuller, *Interpreting the Miracles* (Philadelphia: Westminster, 1963), 55.

6. Ibid., 34.

7. Ibid., 423.

8. William Hendricksen, *New Testament Commentary: Exposition on the Gospel According to Mark* (Grand Rapids, Mich.: Baker Book House,

1975). See also Perry H. Biddle, *Preaching the Lectionary: A Workbook for Year B* (Louisville, Ky.: Westminster/John Knox, 1990).

9. Harlan Lane, *When the Mind Hears: A History of the Deaf* (New York: Random House, 1984), 393.

10. Ibid., 392-94.

11. William Yount, *Be Opened* (Nashville: Broadman, 1976).

12. William Barclay, *The Gospel of Mark*, rev. ed. (Philadelphia: Westminster, 1975), 181.

13. Eduard Schweizer, *The Good News According to Mark* (Atlanta: John Knox, 1977), 154.

14. Barclay, *The Gospel of Mark*, 181.

15. Ched Myers, *Binding the Strong Man* (Maryknoll, N.Y.: Orbis, 1988), 205.

16. Ibid.

17. John Killinger, *Day By Day with Jesus: 365 Meditations on the Gospels* (Nashville: Abingdon, 1994), 136.

18. Ibid.

19. Perry H. Biddle, *Preaching the Lectionary: A Workbook for Year B* (Louisville, Ky.: Westminster/John Knox, 1990), 277.

20. The belief that demon possession was the cause of the man's deafness has its roots in two places. Some scholars believe that the phrase "tongue was released" in verse 35 indicates an "original notion of demonic restraint." See Schweizer, *The Good News According to Mark*, 154. According to this interpretation, the cure is viewed as an exorcism, not a healing. See Fuller, *Interpreting the Miracles*, 423.

21. Leslie C. Mitton, *The Gospel According to St. Mark* (London: Epworth, 1957), 59.

22. Eduard Riegert and Richard H. Hiers, *Proclamation: Pentecost 2— Series B* (Philadelphia: Fortress, 1975), 37.

23. Biddle, *Preaching the Lectionary: A Workbook for Year B*, 278.

24. Mitton, *The Gospel According to St. Mark*, 58.

25. Henry Wilson Steward, *The Speaking God: Luther's Theology of Preaching* (Ann Arbor, Mich.: University Microfilms International, 1977), 121.

26. J. C. Amman, *Dissertatio de Loquelo* (Amsterdam: J. Wolters, 1700). English translation: *A Dissertation on Speech* (1873; reprint, Amsterdam: North Holland, 1965). Quoted in Lane, *When the Mind Hears*, 101.

27. Fred Craddock, *As One Without Authority: Essays on Inductive Preaching* (Nashville: Abingdon, 1979), 31.

28. David G. Buttrick, *Homiletical Moves and Structures* (Philadelphia: Fortress, 1987), 211.

29. Walter Brueggemann, *Finally Comes the Poet: Daring Speech for Proclamation* (Minneapolis: Fortress, 1989), 49.

30. Biddle, *Preaching the Lectionary: A Workbook for Year B*, 278.

31. For a more detailed analysis of preaching's overemphasis on the oral and aural, see Kathleen Black, "Beyond the Spoken Word," *Quarterly Review* (Fall, 1994): 279-93.

32. Riegert and Hiers, *Proclamation: Pentecost 2— Series B*, 40.

33. Halford E. Luccock, exposition to "The Gospel According to St. Mark," in *The Interpreter's Bible* (Nashville: Abingdon, 1951), 7:756-757.

34. Ibid., 757.

# 5. Paralysis

1. Some scholars identify John 5:1-18 as another text describing the healing of a man who is paralyzed, but the paralysis of this man was partial; he says "while I am *making my way* [to the pool], someone else steps down ahead of me" (v. 7). See Peder Borgen, "Miracles of Healing in the New Testament," *Studia Theologica* 35, no. 2: 103.

2. Murray M. Freed, "Traumatic and Congenital Lesions of the Spinal Cord," in *Krusen's Handbook of Physical Medicine and Rehabilitation*, ed. F. J. Kottke and J. F. Lehmann (Philadelphia: W. B. Saunders, 1990), 721.

3. Ibid., 731.

4. Ibid., 718.

5. Ibid.

6. Donald E. Gowan, "Salvation as Healing," *Ex Auditu* 5 (1989): 11.

7. Ibid.

8. See Reginald H. Fuller, *Interpreting the Miracles* (Philadelphia: Westminster, 1963), 50; F. B. Craddock et al., *Preaching the New Common Lectionary: Year B—Advent, Christmas, Epiphany* (Nashville: Abingdon, 1984), 169; Eduard Schweizer, *The Good News According to Mark* (Atlanta: John Knox, 1977), 60; Halford E. Luccock, exposition to "The Gospel According to Mark," in *The Interpreter's Bible* (Nashville: Abingdon, 1951) 7:668.

9. Gowan, "Salvation as Healing," 2.

10. Ibid., 12.

11. Ched Myers, *Binding the Strong Man: A Political Reading of Mark's Story of Jesus* (Maryknoll, N.Y.: Orbis, 1988), 155.

12. Ibid.

13. Schweizer, *The Good News According to Mark*, 61.

14. Myers, *Binding the Strong Man*, 154.

15. Fuller, *Interpreting the Miracles*, 50.

16. Schweizer, *The Good News According to Mark*, 61.

17. Luccock, "Mark," 7:671.

18. Schweizer, *The Good News According to Mark*, 61.

19. Craddock et al., *Preaching the New Common Lectionary: Year—Advent, Christmas, Epiphany*, 169.

20. Luccock, "Mark," 7:671.

21. Fuller, *Interpreting the Miracles*, 51.

22. Perry H. Biddle, *Preaching the Lectionary: A Workbook for Year B* (Louisville, Ky.: Westminster/John Knox, 1990), 92.

23. Marian Soards, Thomas Dozeman, and Kendall McCabe, *Preaching the Revised Common Lectionary: Year B—Advent/Christmas/Epiphany* (Nashville: Abingdon, 1993), 163.

24. William Barclay, *The Gospel of Mark*, rev. ed. (Philadelphia: Westminster, 1975), 47.

25. Allison Fitzsimons and Werner Kelber, *Proclamation: Epiphany— Series B* (Philadelphia: Fortress, 1975), 42.

26. Craddock et al., *Preaching the New Common Lectionary: Year B— Advent, Christmas, Epiphany*, 169.

27. Ibid., 170.

28. Schweizer, *The Good News According to Mark*, 61.

29. Luccock, "Mark," 7:670.

30. Biddle, *Preaching the Lectionary: A Workbook for Year B*, 93.

31. Reginald H. Fuller, *Preaching the New Lectionary* (Collegeville, Minn.: Liturgical Press, 1971), 324.

32. Myers, *Binding the Strong Man*, 156.

# 6. *Leprosy and Chronic Illness*

1. Demon possession will be dealt with in the following chapter.

2. Donald E. Gowan, "Salvation as Healing," *Ex Auditu* 5 (1989): 12.

3. In the lectionary, the story of the woman with the flow of blood is part of a larger pericope (Mark 5:21-43), which also includes the raising of Jairus's daughter. Since the daughter does not have a disability per se but is considered dead, I will discuss the Jairus pericope only with regard to its relation to the story of the healing of the woman with the flow of blood.

4. Hans Hubner, "Unclean and Clean," in *The Anchor Bible Dictionary* (New York: Doubleday, 1992), 6:729.

5. Cecil Roth, ed. "Purity and Impurity, Ritual," *Encyclopaedia Judaica Jerusalem* (New York: Macmillan, 1971), 13:1405.

6. Ibid., 1414.

7. Ibid.

8. John J. Pilch, "Biblical Leprosy and Body Symbolism," *Biblical Theology Bulletin* 11, no. 4 (Oct. 1981): 111.

9. David P. Wright and Richard N. Jones, "Leprosy," in *The Anchor Bible Dictionary* (New York: Doubleday, 1992), 4:281.

10. Roth, "Purity and Impurity, Ritual," 1405.

11. Max Sussman, "Sickness and Disease," in *The Anchor Bible Dictionary* (New York: Doubleday, 1992), 6:738.

12. Ibid., 737.

13. Roth, "Purity and Impurity, Ritual," 1406.

14. Ibid.

15. Ibid., 1405.

16. Jesus spent a large portion of his life with the Qumran community. The "Q Source," which is a list of the sayings of Jesus separate from the Gospels, comes from the Qumran community.

17. Sussman, "Sickness and Disease," 742.

18. Pilch, "Biblical Leprosy and Body Symbolism," 108.

19. Harvey B. Simon, "Leprosy," *Scientific American Medicine* 8, no. 7 (New York: Scientific American, 1994), 18.

20. Kazmierski disagrees. He says "this pericope is not a story about Jesus, but about the leper, the plot centering only momentarily on Jesus, to return once again to the leper, who has now, in his new state of 'cleanness', become a preacher of the Gospel." He also believes that the subject of verse 45 is the leper, not Jesus—that it was the leper who could no longer go into a town openly and had to stay out in the countryside. See Carl R. Kazmierski, "Evangelist and Leper: A Socio-Cultural Study of Mark 1:40-45," *New Testament Studies* 38 (1992): 39-50.

21. C. H. Cave states that "Galileans were a by-word among the Judaean Pharisees for their laxity with regard to the laws of purity." See Cave, "The Leper: Mark 1:40-45," *New Testament Studies* 25 (1979): 245.

22. Ched Myers, *Binding the Strong Man: A Political Reading of Mark's Story of Jesus* (Maryknoll, N.Y.: Orbis, 1988), 153.

23. Allison and Kelber, *Proclamation: Epiphany— Series B*, 37.

24. Halford E. Luccock, exposition to "The Gospel According to St. Mark," in *The Interpreter's Bible* (Nashville: Abingdon, 1951), 7:666.

25. Eduard Schweizer, *The Good News According to Mark* (Atlanta: John Knox, 1977), 58.

26. Michal Wojciechowski, "The Touching of the Leper (Mark 1:40-45)," *Biblische Zeitschrift* 33, no. 1 (April 1988): 115.

27. Schweizer, *The Good News According to Mark*, 58.

28. Kazmierski, "Evangelist and Leper," 45.

29. Ibid., 46.

30. Myers, *Binding the Strong Man*, 153.

31. See Biddle, *Preaching the Lectionary: A Workbook for Year B*, 88.

32. Reginald H. Fuller, *Preaching the New Lectionary* (Collegeville, Minn.: Liturgical Press, 1971), 322.

33. Allison and Kelber, *Proclamation: Epiphany—Series B*, 38.

34. Ibid., 36.

35. Biddle, *Preaching the Lectionary: A Workbook for Year B*, 88.

36. David Rhoads, *Proclamation 5: Series B—Epiphany* (Minneapolis: Augsburg Fortress, 1993), 43-44.

37. Pilch, "Understanding Biblical Healing," 60.

38. Joseph A. Fitzmyer, *The Anchor Bible: The Gospel According to Luke X-XXIV* (Garden City, N.Y.: Doubleday, 1983), 1150.

39. Ibid.

40. Fuller, *Interpreting the Miracles*, 66.

41. Pilch, "Biblical Leprosy and Body Symbolism," 112.

42. Roth, "Purity and Impurity, Ritual," 1408.

43. Pilch, "Understanding Biblical Healing: Selecting an Appropriate Model," 64.

44. Walter Russell Bowie et al., exposition to "The Gospel According to St. Luke," in *The Interpreter's Bible* (Nashville: Abingdon, 1952), 8:298.

45. Marian Soards, Thomas Dozeman, and Kendall McCabe, *Preaching the Revised Common Lectionary: Year A, After Pentecost 2* (Nashville: Abingdon, 1992), 173.

46. David G. Buttrick, *Proclamation 4: Pentecost 3—Series C* (Philadelphia: Fortress, 1988), 18.

47. Toba Schwaber Kerson and Lawrence A. Kerson, *Understanding Chronic Illness: The Medical and Psychological Dimensions of Nine Diseases* (New York: The Free Press, 1985), 2.

48. Ibid., 280-81.

49. Ibid., 279.

50. Ibid.

51. Martin E. Marty, *A Cry of Absence: Reflections for the Winter of the Heart* (San Francisco: Harper & Row, 1983), 143.

52. Kerson and Kerson, *Understanding Chronic Illness*, 278.

53. Ibid., 282.

54. Marla J. Schierling Selvidge, "Mark 5:25-34 and Leviticus 15:19-20: A Reaction to Restrictive Purity Regulations," *Journal of Biblical Literature* 103 (Dec. 1984): 619.

55. Vernon K. Robbins, "The Woman Who Touched Jesus' Garment: Socio-Rhetorical Analysis of the Synoptic Accounts," *New Testament Studies* 33, no. 4 (1987): 511.

56. Mary Ann Tolbert, "The Woman with the Hemorrhage," in *The Women's Bible Commentary*, ed. by Carol A. Newsom and Sharon H. Ringe (Louisville: Westminster/John Knox, 1992), 267.

57. Myers, *Binding the Strong Man*, 199.

58. Tolbert, "The Woman with the Hemorrhage," 268.

59. Robbins, "The Woman Who Touched Jesus' Garment," 504.

60. Ibid., 510, 513.

61. Ibid., 510.

62. Marian Soards, Thoman Dozeman, and Kendall McCabe, *Preaching the Revised Common Lectionary: After Pentecost 1* (Nashville: Abingdon, 1993), 84.

63. Luccock, exposition to "Mark," 720.

# 7. Mental Illness

1. Harold S. Songer, "Demon Possession and Mental Illness," *Religion in Life* 36, no. 1 (spring 1967): 120.

2. Ibid., 121.

3. Ibid., 124.

4. Howard, "New Testament Exorcism and its Significance Today," *Expository Times* 96 (Jan. 1985): 108.

5. Antoinette Clark Wire, "The Structure of the Gospel Miracle Stories and Their Tellers," *Semeia* 11 (1978): 91.

6. Ibid., 109.

7. Letter from the Reverend Meredyth Bellows about her son Einar Sigtier Bellows, 1994.

8. S. Vernon McCasland, *By the Finger of God* (New York: Macmillan, 1951), 26.

9. American Psychiatric Association, *Diagnostic and Statistical Manual of Mental Disorders*, 3d rev. ed. (Washington, D.C.: American Psychiatric Association, 1987), xxiii.

10. Howard, "New Testament Exorcism and Its Significance Today," 108.

11. Dire economic circumstances are changing the statistics daily.

12. This text was one of the few that was first told in Aramaic. See Reginald H. Fuller, *Interpreting the Miracles* (Philadelphia: Westminster, 1963), 34.

13. J. Duncan Derrett, "Contributions to the Study of the Gerasene Demoniac," *Journal for the Study of the New Testament* 3 (1979): 13.

14. William Hendricksen, *New Testament Commentary: Exposition on the Gospel According to Luke* (Grand Rapids, Mich.: Baker Book House, 1975), 450.

15. David L. Tiede, *Augsburg Commentary on the New Testament: Luke* (Minneapolis: Augsburg, 1988), 172.

16. Ched Myers, *Binding the Strong Man: A Political Reading of Mark's Story of Jesus* (Maryknoll, N.Y.: Orbis, 1988), 191.

17. Ibid., 194.

18. Barclay, *The Gospel of Luke*, 108.

19. Myers, *Binding the Strong Man*, 192, 193. See also Paul Hollenbach, "Jesus, Demoniacs, and Public Authorities: A Socio-Historical Study," *The Journal of the American Academy of Religion* 49, no. 4 (1981) 567-88; and Frantz Fanon, *The Wretched of the Earth* (New York: Ballantine, 1963).

20. See Joseph A. Fitzmyer, *The Anchor Bible: The Gospel According to Luke I-IX* (Garden Grove, N.Y.: Doubleday, 1983), 733.

21. Frederick W. Danker, *Jesus and the New Age: A Commentary on Luke's Gospel* (Philadelphia: Fortress, 1988), 181.

22. Myers, *Binding the Strong Man*, 191.

23. Hendricksen, *The New Testament Commentary: Exposition on the Gospel According to Luke*, 446.

24. Johnson, *The Gospel of Luke*, 137.

25. Danker, *Jesus and the New Age*, 183.

26. Ibid.

27. Derrett, "Contributions to the Study of the Gerasene Demoniac," 5.

28. Ibid.

29. Johnson, *The Gospel of Luke*, 137.

30. Danker, *Jesus and the New Age*, 184.

31. Hendricksen, *New Testament Commentary: Exposition on the Gospel According to Luke*, 450.

32. Danker, *Jesus and the New Age*, 184.

33. Howard, "New Testament Exorcism and Its Significance Today," 109.

34. Walter Russell Bowie et al., exposition to "The Gospel According to St. Luke," in *The Interpreter's Bible* (Nashville, Abingdon, 1952), 8:157.

35. Songer, "Demon Possession and Mental Illness," 122.

# 8. *A Healing Homiletic*

1. Excerpted from a sermon written by the Rev. Deborah Lerner in June of 1995. She remembered the illustration from the preaching of the Rev. DeWane Zimmerman, First United Methodist Church, Phoenix, Arizona.

# Scripture Index

Exodus
20:5. . . . . . . . . . . . . . . . . . . . 66
34:7. . . . . . . . . . . . . . . . . . . . 66

Leviticus
11–17 . . . . . . . . . . . . . . . . . . 125
11:44-45 . . . . . . . . . . . . . . . . 125
13:1-46 . . . . . . . . . 129, 130, 136
14:1-32 . . . . . . . 129, 130-31, 136
15:25-30 . . . . . . . . . . . . . . . . 152
19:14. . . . . . . . . . . . . . . . . . . . 88
21:17-23 . . . . . . . . . . . . . . . . . 49
24:16. . . . . . . . . . . . . . . . . . . 117

Numbers
14:18. . . . . . . . . . . . . . . . . . . . 66
19 . . . . . . . . . . . . . . . . . . . . . 125

Deuteronomy
5:9-10 . . . . . . . . . . . . . 24, 26, 66

2 Kings
5:15-27 . . . . . . . . . . . . . 126, 142

2 Chronicles
26:16-21 . . . . . . . . . . . . . . . . 126

Isaiah
29:18. . . . . . . . . . . . . . . . . . . . 88
35:5-6 . . . . . . . . . . . . 88, 98, 124
43:25. . . . . . . . . . . . . . . . . . . 117

Matthew
8:1-4 . . . . . . . . . . . . . . . . . . . 125

8:5-13 . . . . . . . . . . . . . . . . . . 104
8:28-34 . . . . . . . . . . . . . . . . . 159
9:1-8 . . . . . . . . . . . . . . . . . . . 104
9:20-22 . . . . . . . . . . . . . . . . . 125
9:27-31 . . . . . . . . . . . . . . . . . . 57
9:32-34 . . . . . . . . . . . 37, 97, 159
10:8. . . . . . . . . . . . . . . . . . . . 124
11:4-5 . . . . . . . . . . . . . . . 88, 124
12:22-32 . . . . . . . . . 57, 97, 159
15:21-28 . . . . . . . . . . . . . . . . 159
15:30-31 . . . . . . . . . . . . . . . . 104
17:14-21 . . . . . . . . . . . . 124, 159
20:30-34 . . . . . . . . . . . . . . . . . 57
21:14. . . . . . . . . . . . . . . . . . . 104
26:6. . . . . . . . . . . . . . . . . . . . 125

Mark
1:21-28 . . . . . . . . . . . . . . . . . 159
1:40-45 Year B, Epiphany . . . 125
131-40, 141, 143
2:1-12 Year B, Epiphany . . . . . 22
104, 109-23
3:19-30 . . . . . . . . . . . . . . . . . 159
5:1-20 . . . . . . . . . . . . . . . . . . 159
5:25-34 Year B, After Pentecost
(Ordinary Time) . . . . . 22, 125,
150-58
5:41. . . . . . . . . . . . . . . . . . . . 134
7:14-23 . . . . . . . . . . . . . . . . . 128
7:24-30 . . . . . . . . . . . . . . 88, 159
7:31-37 Year B, After Pentecost
(Ordinary Time) . . . . . 65, 88,
92-103, 135
8:22-26 . . . . . . . . . 57, 65, 79, 96

Mark (*continued*)
9:14-29 . . . . . . . . . . 97, 124, 159
10:46-52 *Year B, After Pentecost
(Ordinary Time)* 57, 78-87, 117
14:3. . . . . . . . . . . . . . . . . . . 125

Luke
4:24. . . . . . . . . . . . . . . . . . 175
4:28-29 . . . . . . . . . . . . . . . . 38
4:31-37 . . . . . . . . . . . . . . . 159
5:12-14 . . . . . . . . . . . . . . . 125
5:17-26 . . . . . . . . . . . . . . . 104
6:20-25 . . . . . . . . . . . . . . . . 31
7:1-10 . . . . . . . . . . . . . . . . 104
7:22. . . . . . . . . . . . . . . 88, 124
7:50. . . . . . . . . . . . . . . . . . 113
8:26-39 *Year C, After Pentecost
(Ordinary Time)* . . . . 113, 159,
162, 165-79
8:43-48 . . . . . . . . . . . . . . . 125
9:37-43 . . . . . . . . . . . . 124, 159
9:51. . . . . . . . . . . . . . . . . . 143
11:14. . . . . . . . . . . . . . . . . . 97
11:24. . . . . . . . . . . . . . . . . 167
14:16-24 . . . . . . . . . . . . . . . 21

17:11-19 *Year C, After Pentecost
(Ordinary Time)* . . 125, 141-48
18:35-43 . . . . . . . . . . . . . . . . 57
19:9. . . . . . . . . . . . . . . . . . 113

John
5:3. . . . . . . . . . . . . . . . . . . 104
7:20. . . . . . . . . . . . . . . . . . 159
8:48-52 . . . . . . . . . . . . . . . 159
9:1-41 *Year A, Lent* . . . . 21, 29, 57
60-78, 84, 85, 110
10:19-21 . . . . . . . . . . . . . . . 159
11:14-23 . . . . . . . . . . . . . . . 159

Romans
8:22-26 . . . . . . . . . . . . . . . . 97
10:17. . . . . . . . . . . . . . . . . . 99

1 Corinthians
12:26. . . . . . . . . . . . . . . . . . 38

2 Corinthians
5:2-4 . . . . . . . . . . . . . . . . . . 97
11:25. . . . . . . . . . . . . . . . . . 38
12:9. . . . . . . . . . . . . . . . 21, 29